The

ART OF STUDYING

An Islamic Approach to
Academic Success

The

ART OF STUDYING

An Islamic Approach to
Academic Success

HATEEM SIDDIQUI, M.D.

Requests for authorization should be addressed to
      Email: anislamicapproach@gmail.com
      Facebook: www.facebook.com/anislamicapproach

Cover Arabic Calligraphy by Faran Kharal
Cover Design by Hamza Siddiqui
Interior layout and design by www.writingnights.org
Book preparation by Chad Robertson
Indexer: AElfwine Mischler

ISBN: 9781729075128

Printed in the United States of America.

24   23   22   21   20   19   18   17   8   7   6   5   4   3   2   1

Dedication

To my family and my brothers and sisters in faith,
those who are present and those who will come after me

أَعُوْذُبِاللهِ مِنَ الْشَّيْطَانِ الْرَّجِيْمِ

I seek refuge in Allah from the cursed devil

With the Name of Allah, the Most Merciful, the Most Compassionate

All praise and thanks are due to Allah, the Master and Caretaker of everything

I ask Allah to send His peace and blessings upon Prophet Muhammad ﷺ, his family, his companions, his helpers, and his followers until the Day of Judgment

Contents

Dedication v

Contents vii

Foreword viii

Arabic Words and Abbreviations ix

Acknowledgements xi

Introduction Read! Reviving The Spirit Of Study 1

1 The Power of Intention 15

2 Keep Moving Forward 27

3 A Light at the End of the Tunnel 39

4 Patience and Prayer 49

5 An Answered Supplication 69

6 Toward Seeking Forgiveness 95

7 An Attitude of Gratefulness 111

8 Balance 125

9 Time Management 147

10 One Step at a Time 165

11 Strive for Excellence 177

12 Tie Your Camel 199

13 Contentment 213

14 Trust the Process 223

Conclusion 232

About the Author 237

Index 239

Foreword

Narrated 'Umar ibn al-Khattab (رضي الله عنه):

The Messenger of Allah (ﷺ) said, "The deeds are considered by the intentions, and a person will get the reward according to his intention. So whoever emigrated for Allah and His Messenger, his emigration will be for Allah and His Messenger; and whoever emigrated for worldly benefits or for a woman to marry, his emigration would be for what he emigrated for".

RIYADH AS SALIHEEN BOOK 1 HADITH #1
(SAHIH AL-BUKHARI, SAHIH MUSLIM)

Arabic Words and Abbreviations

Allah: the name of the one God in Arabic

ﷺ: *(sallā Allāhu ʿalayhi wa-sallam):* Arabic phrase used when mentioning Prophet Muhammad that means "Peace and blessings be upon him"

Qur'an: the speech of Allah collected into the holy book of the Muslims

surah: a "chapter" of the Qur'an, which is comprised of 114 chapters

sunnah (plural sunan): the way of life prescribed for Muslims based on the Qur'an and *hadith*

hadith: the Prophet's ﷺ sayings, actions, and approvals, along with descriptions of his physical attributes, manners, and conduct; books of hadith that are mentioned in this book include *Sahih Al-Bukhari, Sahih Muslim, Sunan Abi Dawud, Jamiʿ at-Tirmidhi, Sunan ibn Majah, Sunan an-Nasai, Riyadh as Saliheen,* and *Muwatta Malik,* in addition to those otherwise noted.

inshaAllah: Arabic term used for future events, meaning, "By the will of Allah"

alhamdulillah: Arabic term meaning, "All praise and thanks are due to Allah."

subhanAllah: Arabic term meaning, "Glorified be Allah."

Ramadan: the ninth month of the Islamic lunar calendar, which is a month of fasting as well as the month in which the Qur'an was revealed

رضي الله عنه *(radiAllahu ʿanhu):* an honorific meaning, "May Allah be pleased with him," which, along with the following two, is used most commonly when referring to the companions of the Prophet ﷺ

رضي الله عنها *(radiAllahu ʿanha):* "May Allah be pleased with her."

رضي الله عنهم *(radiAllahu ʿanhum):* "May Allah be pleased with them."

عليه السلام *(ʿalayhi as-salaam):* an honorific meaning, "Peace be upon him," which is used after mentioning prophets.

Acknowledgements

Abu Hurairah رضي الله عنه reported that the Prophet ﷺ said:

"He has not thanked Allah who has not thanked people."[1]

After *Allah*, to whom all praise and thanks belongs, I must thank my parents for instilling in me—among many good things—faith, strong work ethic, and good morals. Their supplications for me and their support for me are the stepping stones for whatever success comes after. Thereafter, my wife for her patience, love, and support throughout the writing of this book.

I do not profess to be a scholar of religion, let alone Islam. Therefore, there are many people who have been integral in forming this book, directly and indirectly, through the wealth of Islamic knowledge that is being disseminated through the various avenues in the information age. To

---

[1] *Sunan Abi Dawud* #4811

move forward without recognizing them, thanking them, and asking Allah to bless them would be a mistake. Therefore, I take this moment to also acknowledge them directly.

I have relied heavily, of course, on the *Qur'an* and the authentic *Sunnah.* Thereafter, I relied on the classical works of Imam Al-Ghazali and Imam Ibn Al-Qayyim, both of whom are giants in the topic of spiritual purification. However, the gems from these works became accessible to me through the teachers of the present day, namely, Ustadh Hassan Elwan, Dr. Imad Bayoun, Ustadh Nouman Ali Khan, Sheikh Yasir Qadhi, Sheikh Omar Suleiman, Imam Suhaib Webb, and countless others, whose advice help shape the central messages of some of the chapters of this book.

In addition, Internet resources such as *Quran.com, Sunnah.com, Islamqa,* as well as many other websites that are too numerous to name have been invaluable in referencing these texts and for general accessibility to sacred knowledge for the layman. I have quoted each source as diligently as possible in the footnotes and used the common numbering method for *hadith* (by quoting the hadith number) which is also available on Sunnah.com, so that it is easily accessible to anyone to access on the Internet for further review. Translations for Qur'an are from Sahih International and hadith translations are as sourced on Sunnah.com for the individual hadith books, but sometimes other translations are used for readability purposes (without changing the intended meaning of the text). I especially encourage the reader in their leisure to examine Qur'an and hadith that are not directly quoted in this text to benefit from their gems.

I am also indebted to my advisor in reviewing this book for accuracy within the Islamic tradition, Ustadh Hassen Morad (graduate from Al-Azhar University), who patiently worked with me in correcting mistakes and ensuring accuracy in explaining Islamic concepts. I am also thankful to my copyeditor Sharon Honeycutt, who through her professional editing experience improved this book's readability and improved my writing in preparation for publication. I would also like to acknowledge my proofreaders, Jeff Rudolph and Iesha Javed, who ensured that my writing was as mistake-free as possible and allowed me to present a refined text. Other contributors to this book, including for the cover art, book design, and index are mentioned in the title pages.

If there is anything beneficial that is a result of this book, then know it is from Allah. Whatever mistakes may be present are from my own shortcomings, and I ask Allah to forgive me for any mistakes.

Lastly, I ask Allah to bless, protect, and forgive all of our teachers, scholars, workers, students, and their families and to reward them with the best in this life and the Hereafter. If I have failed to mention anyone specifically I ask Allah to include them in this supplication.

Introduction

Read!
Reviving The Spirit Of Study

Fear is a powerful emotion that leads to behavioral changes that begin in the mind and flow to the rest of the body, inevitably mobilizing people in a certain direction. Fear can be used as a catalyst or as a roadblock. In different times and places throughout human history, prominent leaders instilled fear into their followers and found that it was a more-than-adequate catalyst to enact change. However, many today cite fear as the primary roadblock to their ability to complete tasks, enact change, and achieve their dreams

Our experiences with fear, whether as a catalyst or a roadblock, can be negative or positive, or even somewhere in between. For example, fear as a roadblock can be positive when our fear of burning our finger forces us to think twice before touching a hot pan on the stove. In contrast, fear as a roadblock can be negative if we have built irrational fears around studying (resulting, perhaps, from a previous negative experience, such as failing) that demoralize us and prevent us from pursuing a difficult degree. Fear as a catalyst can also function as a positive or a negative based on our past experiences. However, it is not the experiences themselves, but our *perception* of the experiences that produces a reaction. In other words, our perception of fear either mobilizes and motivates us toward removing the objects that cause fear, or it paralyzes us and impedes our forward progress.

During my years of pursuing my own education, I have noticed that many of us have indirectly created a culture of irrational fear around studying, school, and especially exams. This is no surprise, since education has been reduced simply to a means toward a career rather than an enjoyable pursuit, a trivialization that has many consequences.

One specific consequence is that serious studying is only done near the time of the exam. Why is this? These tests determine our grades and ultimately our careers, so anticipating them may cause anxiety in us, turning studying into an object of fear because of its potential negative consequences (e.g., failing, repeating a class, not advancing in our career, potential stigma), systematically reducing studying from a noble pursuit to a loathsome activity that is highly unenjoyable. As a result, we think of studying as something that inhibits us from doing what "we really want to do." This process of fear and loathing has led us to one of the worst, most prevalent habits of our generation: procrastination.

Most students develop bad habits early. Paramount among these bad habits is procrastination, but they also include (and are not limited to) cramming a semester's coursework into finals week, "all-nighters," spending more time on breaks than on studying, calculating the lowest possible grade to pass a class, and doing everything other than studying during our dedicated study time—none of which are new phenomena. Given the stimulus of fear and the negative perception of partaking in a loathsome activity that has potential negative consequences, humans will always find something else to do. In the past it was arm wrestling or playing cards or board games; today, we have more complex, time-consuming distractions with the advent of the Internet, social media, and video gaming. None of these pastimes are inherently "evil," but the worth of a hobby or pastime is determined by our experience, perception, and the outcomes of these activities. Many times these benign hobbies become our object of comfort in times of fear (in order to avoid work, for example) and in the future become addictions instead of healthy outlets in which we can relax away from strenuous work.

I write about these phenomena because I was very well a part of this culture. After many years and many near-failures, I realized that Islamic habits also contribute toward success in the secular realm, enabling me to succeed where I previously failed. Subsequently, Allah allowed me to enjoy many successes: from scoring in the highest percentile on board exams and being recognized as a top medical resident during training, to practicing as a board-certified physician. The path was not easy, but the stories along the way and the lessons learned inspired much of the central advice in this book.

Although I was a valedictorian of my high school class, the study habits I developed during that time nearly resulted in failed classes at the upper-degree levels. In high school, studying the day before the test was usually enough to allow me to pass the class with flying colors—not because of my perceived intelligence, but because the system was woefully inadequate in preparing students for a lifetime of learning. This trend unfortunately continued into my undergraduate career.

While I got by for the first couple years, as I advanced, I realized that I was not as intelligent as I thought I was. My bad habits (chief of which was procrastination) allowed significant amounts of coursework to pile up. As my extracurricular activities and responsibilities outside school increased (for example, studying Islam and trying to get closer to Allah, taking up leadership positions in the Muslim Students Association, traveling to different campuses to work with other Muslim organizations, and volunteering in the hospital), I soon became so overwhelmed with the amount of material I had to learn that, for the first time in my student life, I struggled to keep up in my classes.

Toward the end of my undergraduate career, my general inattentiveness, long nights doing anything but studying, and skipping class put me on the brink of failure. To illustrate, consider what I did to barely pass my embryology class my senior year: For an extra-credit assignment the night before it was due, I used clips from the *Lion King* (in Spanish) to creatively explain fetal development, learned how to compile a video in Windows Movie Maker, scrambled for a missing USB to which I could transfer the video, relied on a friend to drive me to the school library to upload the video the following day (since our Internet access was slow) and anxiously waited for the video to upload to YouTube just minutes before the deadline.

During this chaotic time, I was also studying for the MCAT (the Medical College Admission Test). My parents shelled out an enormous amount of money for me to be placed in a review course that would help prepare me to score well in order to secure a seat in a coveted U.S. medical school. In the end, despite the expensive course and using the same habits that brought me success in the past, I struggled and essentially failed the MCAT, which effectively took me out of the running for a U.S. medical school education. Because of the tremendous guilt I felt, being unable to translate the success I had in high school to my undergraduate career, failing the MCAT, and not getting into a U.S. medical school, I skipped my graduation ceremony entirely, causing my parents pain as they could not fully celebrate the first child in the family to complete college in the U.S.

As I look back at these times in my life, I find that what I feared most actually came true. My fear of failing did not act as a catalyst for change; rather, it became a roadblock. I sought comfort in my hobbies until they became addictions, consuming precious time that I could have used for studying and succeeding. Thus, fear led to procrastination, which inevitably damaged my chances of getting into medical school, which tremendously changed my pathway to becoming a physician. Despite this humbling experience, I did not truly learn my lesson until I nearly failed anatomy in medical school abroad. The potential ramifications of failing were daunting: a repeated semester, increased financial burden, and the potential negative stigma I would feel from my family, friends, and cohorts.

Fortunately, through the help of honest colleagues, I realized not only that my study habits were painfully deficient, but that I did not know *how* to study at all. Throughout my life as a student, I had cheated the system and rode near the top of the class—despite bad habits and minimal effort (this is probably a failure of the educational system in conjunction with my own weaknesses, but that is a separate issue beyond the scope of this book). The daunting challenges of my final years of college and the beginning of medical school forced me to learn a valuable lesson: it was no longer feasible to leave everything to the very end. This is true for any high-level degree, because the amount of material that needs to be mastered is so vast and relevant to our career paths that it requires more sincere dedication. In medical school, excuses such as "the prerequisite classes have nothing to do with my field" were no longer valid. I needed to rectify my study habits and face my fears directly.

As I alluded to prior, I had become quite active within the Muslim community during this turbulent time, actively participating and volunteering in events while trying to cultivate my own education within the Islamic field. Of course, the latter required a significant amount of time that I did not have because of the demands of the coursework for school. And so came the days where balancing my student life, social life, and "Islamic life" became difficult, and the stark realization that something had to be sacrificed came to a head. But I was not alone. My colleagues were also struggling with this balance, and each chose a different part of their life to sacrifice.

During my time in school, I noticed a stark dichotomy between competing groups of Muslim students. The first was a group that had nothing to do with Islam and sacrificed its tenets for the benefit of added study time in order to do well in school. The second group were so entrenched in the pursuit of becoming better Muslims that their time for study was severely limited, leading to difficulty excelling in school. In other words, the "religious" people were struggling in school and the "nonpracticing" people were doing better. Unfortunately, as I began my own journey to learn better study habits, I found that dedicating more time to studying for school often interfered with my progression of becoming a better Muslim.

Faced with this dilemma of choosing between two extremes, I asked myself a question:

What study habits contribute to studying better and getting better results?

Fortunately, this was answered by my friends and honest colleagues who mentored me by promoting good study habits (which I will mention later in this book). But the problem of sacrificed time for religious studies was still evident, so I asked a follow-up question:

Are there Islamic means to developing better study habits?

Asking this question enabled me to reflect on Islamic concepts in new ways and to correlate them to school, helping me to cope with the loathsome activity of studying and to perceive it in a healthier way. Specifically, I started to *apply* the abstract Islamic concepts I had learned to my day-to-day life. Because of this exercise in humility—of being brought down after initial success—I realized Islam can develop a person into a better student without having to sacrifice anything from studying at all.

To elaborate, there are spiritual means and worldly means for obtaining everything we want and going wherever we want to go. The problem is we often focus so much on the worldly means by relying on our own ability, our teachers' or friends' abilities, and the ability of review courses that we forget the valuable spiritual means that can *bless* these worldly means. We exhaust all of these worldly means first, and only after failing do we inevitably come back to Allah, essentially placing Him last on our list to rely on. Infusing Islamic concepts into my study habits taught me that success is recognized when we place Allah first and *then* proceed to studying.

But before speaking further about the specific Islamic tools that enabled me to improve my study habits, it is first necessary to foster a positive mindset; in so doing, we aim revive the spirit of study within our legacy. It is to change everything that is negative about studying and exams and reflect on its positivity and our innate ability to tackle any challenge. This positive mindset transforms studying from a boring chore to a pursuit of knowledge that will not only help us obtain careers, but also learned minds. It helps us reflect on the great blessing that Allah bestowed upon us that other people only wish they had but cannot access. This positive mindset helps us do something meaningful with the opportunity we have been given, preventing us from letting ourselves live less than our potential, and from letting down ourselves, our community, and the people who wish they were in our places.

The negative feelings we harbor about studying ultimately lead to stressful days leading up to exams, general unhappiness, and possibly failing altogether. Negative feelings about the process inevitably lead to complaining, which decreases our resolve and leads to self-doubt, resulting in unhealthy study habits and culminating in substandard performances on our exams.

Instead, think positive thoughts. Don't settle for the prevailing culture of pulling all-nighters and letting stress overwhelm you. Being positive means to imagine our success before it happens, ignore negative thoughts, and abandon a culture of complaining. This approach enables us to work on our self-confidence and build a steady resolve that leads to discipline, a good plan, and better study habits, all of which contribute to better grades and success. When we do that, we allow ourselves to learn fresh approaches to studying, finish our studying in a fraction of the time and retain more information, and even have a few spare hours to enjoy ourselves. The power of positivity naturally attracts and breeds further success, and as we explore later in this book, it is a key, forgotten quality of Muslim character.

Another forgotten quality of the Muslim is the pursuit of education. All knowledge is from Allah. Consider that the first commandment to the Prophet Muhammad ﷺ—who was unlettered—was *"iqra"* or "Read!" It was a commandment that was revealed to a society that had not yet left any enduring impact on the world, that was divided into warring tribes without any unifying identity and was technologically backward, but later invigorated the same hearts toward education, eventually developing into the most learned civilization of their time. Consider that it was the Muslims who preserved the knowledge of antiquity by translating that knowledge into Arabic while simultaneously contributing to the development of the scientific method, advancing the study of mathematics, astronomy, and medicine. Thus, when Allah states:

Recite in the name of your Lord who created –
Created man from a clinging substance,[2]

He commands us to education (all types, though seeking Islamic education is the highest branch) *with* His help and support.

And He continues:

Recite, and your Lord is the most Generous
Who taught by the pen –
Taught man that which he knew not.[3]

To illustrate the power of the pen in benefiting and disseminating knowledge.

As I compiled and wrote about the top Islamically inspired tools that enable the Muslim to develop into a better student, the message became clear: to be successful and revive the legacy of our community as torch bearers in secular and religious education, we need to remind ourselves that reading (or education) can be combined with the pursuit of the love of Allah by seeking His help. With time, I discovered that more and more people were receptive to this idea and were struggling with the same balance. This topic ultimately became the most popular post on my personal

---

[2] Qur'an Chapter 96 (*The Clinging Substance*), verses 1–2. It is interesting to note that Allah uses the word *"alaq"* ("clinging substance") to describe the creation of man to the premodern world. We know now through modern advances in embryology that when the fertilized egg enters the uterus, it in fact *clings* to the uterine wall.
[3] Qur'an Chapter 96 (*The Clinging Substance*), verses 3–5

blog, furthering my conviction that it was important to provide this resource to the community. I pray that it will be a source of benefit for my brothers and sisters who are struggling with studying and hope it will help us to see a better path—a path in which we do not need to sacrifice our religion to be better students, a path upon which we can combine religion and the worldly life and be successful in both.

These Islamic tools are by no means new. They are praiseworthy habits in Islam that will aid students in their journeys and are presented in a form that may be more accessible than learning the concepts in a more traditional way. Moreover, this book aims to present the virtuous character of an ideal Muslim and seeks to specifically address them with regards to studying.

Due to the nature of the advice, I find that it will be most beneficial, *inshaAllah* to the Muslim, but perhaps those of other faiths (or no faith) can find some benefit in this advice as well, as they are noble virtues to which morally inclined people are attracted. Further, this advice is primarily geared toward high school, undergraduate, and graduate students, but can be applied by anyone, young and old, who seek betterment for themselves or their children, *inshaAllah*.

As for what follows, they are the lessons that I learned and applied from Islam and infused into my study habits throughout the next phases of my medical career and life—in other words, *The Art of Studying from an Islamic Approach*. They are what helped me enjoy numerous successes with the help of Allah, including scoring in the highest percentile of each medical licensing exam and allowing me to become a board-certified physician. They are the lessons that completely changed my mindset regarding studying, thereby transforming my perception of it from a loathsome activity to an activity that strengthens faith and life. I hope these lessons may help us become better students and better people, and ultimately, change the culture of fear around studying, motivating us to reach our highest aspirations, reminding us of the blessed legacy, and helping us contribute to the revival of Muslim scholarship.

Narrated 'Umar ibn al-Khattab (رضي الله عنه):

The Messenger of Allah (ﷺ) said, "The deeds are considered by the intentions, and a person will get the reward according to his intention. So whoever emigrated for Allah and His Messenger, his emigration will be for Allah and His Messenger; and whoever emigrated for worldly benefits or for a woman to marry, his emigration would be for what he emigrated for".

RIYADH AS SALIHEEN BOOK 1 HADITH #1
(SAHIH AL-BUKHARI, SAHIH MUSLIM)

1

The Power of Intention

The "Power of Intention" is a popular concept made famous by the late motivational author Dr. Wayne Dyer, and although the ideas he imparted regarding intention were borrowed from antiquity, its prevalence in the present is palpable. Intention is also central to the discussion regarding the art of studying from an Islamic perspective and is the first concept we will review.

Many Muslims probably could have guessed that intention was going to be one of the topics of this book—or, in fact, any book that seeks to develop Islamic character. It is so widely spoken about that sometimes we consider it cliché and take the advice for granted, allowing ourselves to forget how central intention is to our lives. It is so central, in fact, that some scholars have commented that the hadith of intention (quoted at the beginning of the chapter) comprises one-third of knowledge. Imam al-Bayhaqi explains that this is because intention represents one-third of all possible actions from which people can attain good deeds—specifically, an action of the heart (the other actions being of the limb and the tongue).[4] Many early scholars were so keen to pay attention to the advice contained in the hadith of intention that they specifically started their books with this hadith; *Sahih al-Bukhari* is a good example.

Just as we perform external deeds with our limbs, we also perform deeds with our heart, and one of the most important deeds of the heart is making an intention. Be mindful, however, that every action is judged by its intention. Intention can also be thought of as the *purpose* of the action, the driving force that helps a person actualize what they are trying to do and that creates visionaries who look past the present experiences on the road to achieving their goals. Intention is what Allah examines when evaluating the sincerity of an action, so much so that it is the major determinant of the acceptance of the action; since intention leads to action, it is only natural to judge the action by its original intent. The added benefit, however, is that because of the pureness of the original intention, our imperfection as human beings (i.e. not being able to complete the intended action) can potentially be overlooked by Allah. The implication is that, because of the pureness of the intention, we may be able to earn the reward of completing a project even if the project was never completed.

As Muslims, we are encouraged to constantly evaluate our intentions—*Why am I doing what I'm doing? Why should I choose decision A over decision B?*—and we are constantly forced to make many different decisions in our lives. The major determinants in making a specific decision

---

[4] Jamaal al-Din M. Zarabozo. *Commentary on the forty hadith of An-Nawawi*, 98

start with thinking about the potential risks and benefits of our actions. In other words, we weigh risk-reward and usually choose the easier option with the best results. While most of the time this is probably commendable, it can be detrimental at times—for example, an employee of a successful company choosing to perform the least amount of work while riding their colleagues' coattails. Not only is this detrimental to the individual, as they may never improve, it is also detrimental both to their colleagues who pick up the extra slack and to their company, which will suffer from their laziness.

Another potential reason we may choose a certain path is to arrogantly show off that we are able to complete a certain task. For example, we may choose to study hard to be at the top of our class simply to be at the top of the class and be recognized for that. Thus, the result of all our hard work for the semester will be for that singular recognition and whatever accolades come with it, but we will suffer a lack of long-term fulfillment as we placed our happiness and purpose into temporary goals and recognition.

The hadith of intention has profound implications. Namely, Allah may bless and reward ordinary, permissible actions when our worldly intention is combined with seeking His pleasure. I contend that performing actions while keeping Allah in mind leads to a more balanced approach to life. For example, studying hard while seeking the pleasure of Allah benefits the Muslim both in the worldly sense (by being at the top of the class) and, at the same time, in a spiritual sense by gaining reward from Allah because of their intention. However, in the eventuality that they do not get to the top of the class, the believer does not walk away from this trial empty-handed (as opposed to the one who does not seek Allah in this regard) as they will still have secured a reward with Allah.

Motivation is a difficult emotion to summon each and every day if the purpose of an action—or intention—is not clear. If a student uses only external factors (money, cars, fame, etc.) as their main source of motivation, they will not be able to rise each day and make the necessary changes to achieve their goals. This is because, while it seems in the temporary sense that a person will achieve happiness when they acquire these materials, an important part of their heart will always remain empty and yearn for something more because external realities are temporary, not a means to true happiness and long-term fulfillment. The real motivation should come from within—an internal drive, leading with the pleasure of Allah, but also a drive to do it for yourself, for your parents, or for your community. Internal motivators hold greater worth because we inherently value them. When we combine our motivation with objects we value, nothing can hinder us from achieving our desired goals.

To realize the importance of linking our intention to Allah, one must learn the *ability* of Allah, for the one who knows Allah will value their relationship with Him. Once a person realizes the value of their relationship with Allah, they will begin to motivate themselves to complete any task because not only is this an effective internal motivator, it is also the best motivator.

How does one make an intention?

Intention is the constant battle in our hearts and minds to connect our action to purpose. From the Islamic perspective, it is the active participation of the believer in reflecting on each and every action that they undertake. By cementing the intention first, every potential action is connected with Allah in the highest spiritual sense. Because of this, the believer will find many benefits because their work is blessed; for example, they may find their work easier than they initially perceived it would be. When a person practices this type of mindfulness, they connect their intentions to intangible ideals to which every human being naturally gravitates and hopes to implement, perhaps winning the hearts of the people at the same time.

For students, it means we should always ask ourselves, "Why are we studying?" and seek to connect it with a higher purpose. Some of my peers studied to help people, and while this is a noble ambition, it is only temporary, and they are at risk for burnout. Some studied simply to become rich, and while this is not an inherently evil personal ambition, it is also only temporary. Once a temporary goal is fulfilled, it ceases to have the same value it had before we fulfilled it, and we cease to work with the same fervor. Therefore, a student working only toward temporary goals will always look for some other temporary place to put their happiness.

In contrast, the farsighted student chooses to study to please Allah, winning in the short- and long-term. By connecting intention to a higher purpose, they derive silent motivation toward completing their tasks on the way to achieving their goals. But because pleasing Allah is a lifelong journey, they will continue to elevate themselves and find new ways to seek Him. The process serves to encourage constant improvement; the one who practices this will not be pleased with temporary advances, but will seek to aim ever higher, even after reaching their goals.

The intention to "please Allah" sounds wonderful in theory, but a struggling student may question how this is actually practical. One way to overcome this mental block is by compelling ourselves to think about what pleases Allah and then connecting it to our line of work and our goals. For example, Allah is pleased by those who are just in their dealings; a person could study law to please Allah by being just with the oppressed by defending them in writing and speech. Similarly, Allah loves that we take care of the needy; one could study social work to help the underserved in the community. And as a final example, Allah loves the people who teach the Qur'an; one could study it, teach it, and implement its message.

In this way, we link every action that we perform to something greater, and this gives us motivation to push through the mundane experiences on the way to achieving our goals. Intention can be at the most microscopic level. For example, a person who wants to go into medicine could form an intention such as, "I am studying for this calculus exam so that I can get a good grade so that I may be able to attend a prestigious college so that I can study medicine to please Allah by helping the underserved in my community."[5] Thus the math test becomes a necessary stepping stone on the student's path, rather than an obstacle and a source of negativity, and studying for that exam transforms itself from a bothersome activity into an activity that has tangible purpose in both the short- and

---

[5] Note we do not need to state the intention out loud before doing a certain task; it is a statement of the heart with a general inclination to that intention. The intent is important, not the words that go about describing that intent. Additionally, it does not need to be as detailed as described above; a general reminder through mindfulness of the original intention in that some tasks are the stepping stones to achieving the ultimate goal of the intention can suffice.

long-term. It should be noted that the intention can be continuously re-
newed, constantly reviewed, and meticulously edited, for as long as we are
performing the actions that are driving us to our end goal. In fact, this
type of behavior should be encouraged because inevitably we will encounter days when it will be very difficult to find our motivation or when we
lose sight of the ultimate reason we are doing anything (for the sake of
Allah).

If we expand this concept further, we arrive at a point where almost
any nonreligious experience in life can be transformed into a good deed
and almost any nonreligious action an act of worship. This is a life of
purpose, and the purpose of life for the Muslim is to worship Allah, as He
states:

> *"And remind, for indeed, the reminder benefits the*
> *believers.*
> *And I did not create the jinn and mankind except to*
> *worship Me."[6]*

Hence, the practicing Muslim would feel less dismayed that they are
not able to compete with their cohorts—who perhaps may have more free
time to perform more of the highly commendable ritual aspects of the
faith (such as voluntary prayers)—for they are at least able to keep pace
somewhat by transforming their daily living and responsibility to good
deeds and spiritual acts by actively practicing their intention. To illustrate

---

[6] Qur'an Chapter 51 ("*The Winnowing Winds*"), verse 55–56

this concept, it was narrated by Abu Mas'ud al-Ansari رضي الله عنه that the Prophet ﷺ said:

> *"When a Muslim spends something on his family intending to receive Allah's reward it is regarded as Sadaqah[7] for him."*[8]

Some of us may struggle with the purpose of creation being the worship of Allah because we equate "worship" only with ritual. While the best forms of worship are the rituals that have been made obligatory (for example, prayer, fasting, charity, pilgrimage, etc.), worship is not exclusive to these. The keen student, using the power of intention, can transform every homework assignment, assigned reading, class sign-in, and exam to an act of worship. Combining these with the obligatory rituals (which they should fulfill regardless), this student can perhaps become a beloved of Allah while reaping the rewards of this world and the Hereafter.

Thus, each day, each time we sit down to study or attend class, we should remember that we are going through that struggle to please Allah, worshipping Him through seeking knowledge. If there are added benefits—such as helping people in need or becoming a successful Muslim in a respectable career, for instance—those are secondary gains. Though we may find it difficult to meditate on this concept and compel our hearts to think this way, it is a necessary exercise that requires practice and diligence. One must not be discouraged if they cannot perfect the intention

---

[7] Originating from the word *sidq* meaning truthfulness, usually understood as sincere voluntary charity

[8] *Sahih al-Bukhari* #5351

right away. Similarly, one must not be deluded into thinking that they should abandon their good deeds and lofty aspirations simply because they think their intention may not be pure. Nay, work hard, dream big, continue to fine-tune your intention, and trust Allah to help you.

If the goal of intention is to please Allah, then what accompanies the intention and the actions that follow is *ikhlas.*[9] Sincerity is the necessary partner of a sound intention, and both comprise the foundation of what the believer stands upon when their actions are complete. Therefore, be careful to make the foundation pure so that the actions that follow are blessed, as it is this foundation that saves us from ourselves, from becoming arrogant and showing off. Be mindful to start your study sessions with a renewal of your intention and a reminder to try your best to be sincere in front of Allah. Study for His sake and not for anyone else, and you will begin to see a difference in the *quality* of your studying.

Consider the example of Khalid ibn al-Waleed رضي الله عنه, the famous companion of the Prophet ﷺ and a master general and honorable warrior. After a string of improbable victories against the superpowers of Persia and Byzantium, some of the Muslims who followed him felt that they were winning their battles because of Khalid's military prowess and his mere presence in their ranks. In response, the leader of the faithful 'Umar ibn al-Khattab رضي الله عنه removed Khalid from his command post, fearing that the people had forgotten that victory results only from Allah. Being removed from any position of success or leadership is a test of humility, a litmus test of sincerity, and an opportunity to renew the in-

---

[9] Arabic word referring to sincerity in action and intention

tention. Khalid's response was a testament to all of these qualities in the highest sense, as he continued to fight in the army (though not as the official commander) with the same—if not even stronger—fervor.

Intention is such a powerful tool for the Muslim that it must lead to results. When we shift our intention from the temporary rewards that the world offers to a more profitable approach by worshipping Allah by committing to studying for His sake, we renounce our ego and surrender to His will. When that shift occurs, do we really think Allah will let us down? It is easy for Allah to make what we study easy for us, and it is easy for Him to grant *anyone* success. Perhaps when we realize the power of intention, we will realize that intention is powerful enough that Allah can change our reality, enabling us to move forward in the face of any difficulty on the way to short- and long-term fulfillment.

"Allah does not charge a soul except [with that within] its capacity. It will have [the consequence of] what [good] it has gained, and it will bear [the consequence of] what [evil] it has earned. 'Our Lord, do not impose blame upon us if we have forgotten or erred. Our Lord, and lay not upon us a burden like that which You laid upon those before us. Our Lord, and burden us not with that which we have no ability to bear. And pardon us; and forgive us; and have mercy upon us. You are our protector, so give us victory over the disbelieving people.'"

QUR'AN CHAPTER 2 ("THE COW"): VERSE 286

2

Keep Moving Forward

In whatever situation you find yourself, know that Allah can get you through it. This belief is essential as we progress to higher levels of learning and the burdens of studying become so heavy sometimes that we feel we cannot press forward.

Personally, studying and practicing medicine have meant constant sacrifice and struggle, which became progressively more difficult as the years sped by. Many times, finals would intersect with the fast of *Ramadan*, or in the heat of the summer, in the middle of a move, in between speaking engagements, or among joyous family gatherings. Sacrificing one for the other meant disturbing my friends' and family's happiness for the "reward" of extra study time, which would undoubtedly affect my personal happiness. Additionally, every course's final exam (the final determinants of an entire semester of study) would commonly be held on the same day for hours at a time, which would further test my patience and resolve.

One semester stands out during my education. The morning of finals was first interrupted by electrical outages followed by a pipeline problem that resulted in no running water. Everyone arrived to the exam hall annoyed, and some even arrived late because they missed their alarm. As I observed my colleagues and their long list of complaints, I reflected on my past experiences in Pakistan, where electrical and water outages were the norm instead of a freak occurrence. Allah granted me patience with this trial via my past experiences with this same burden; I had already realized my potential in this situation during my visits to Pakistan. The words of Allah were unshakeable from my mind—that He would not allow such a situation if we were not able to bear it.

In other words, it wasn't a big deal. I had already experienced the heat of summer without a fan or air conditioning and mornings with no water to wash my face. These experiences were unrelated to studying, but they were useful because I was now passing through a similar experience as a student during finals. Thus, the burden of having experienced water and electrical outages in Pakistan was meaningful in that it helped me deal with similar instances in the future. After all, this was only a slight inconvenience in a world of inconveniences. Despite not having electricity or water for the night preceding and the morning of my finals, I had a roof over my head and my health to be thankful for. I was safe from any military advance and from economic hardship. Moreover, if we were to reflect on the burdens of our brothers and sisters in Earth's war-torn lands, we would quickly realize our burdens pale in comparison.

Thus, Allah will never task us with anything we are not able to complete, and He will never place us in a situation we are not able to overcome. True, it helps when we have gone through a similar experience in the past, but whether we have experienced similar burdens or not is irrelevant; it is the *fact* that we are able to bear any challenge placed in front of us. Allah has mentioned this fact in many places in the Qur'an, but perhaps most famously in the final verse of Chapter 2:

> *"On no soul does Allah place a burden they are*
> *unable to complete ..."*[10]

This statement grants the believer hope in desperate times while at the same time empowers them with a positive attitude to keep moving forward through every hardship and burden they experience. Contrast this with someone who does not have the faith, confidence, or hope that they can bear a burden. The burden then becomes a source of grief, so they avoid it, leading to procrastination and a fear of the dreaded inevitability of failure. Instead of working toward removing the burden, they instead blame the One who tested them with the burden. We blame the teacher for the unfair exam instead of blaming ourselves for being unprepared. We breed a culture of fear and annoyance, instead of hope and happiness.

Regarding "unfair" teachers, it is reasonable to address this issue as a legitimate burden students sometimes face in their studies. To be paired with a teacher that we have trouble understanding (e.g., their inability to

---

[10] Qur'an Chapter 2 ("*The Cow*"), verse 286

explain difficult concepts in simple terms or our difficulty in understanding their speech) will test our patience not just with the coursework, but also as we contemplate if it is even worth attending class. To counteract this problem, we must adopt our true role as students: to respect knowledge and the teacher as the master of that knowledge and to learn something from them, even if it is not the actual coursework.

In other words, we endeavor to focus on the positive aspects of the situation and attempt to take something positive from even negative experiences. Metaphorically, we marvel at the intricate web of a spider rather than being afraid of its potential poison. Socially, we learn from others' mistakes rather than gossip about them. And as students, we look past the thick accent of a teacher and marvel at their courage to teach a complicated concept to university-level students in a language that is not their first—learning instead about courage and sacrifice, perhaps reminding ourselves of our teacher's example the next time we are nervous in a public-speaking engagement. Learn then about courage and sacrifice; the textbook will always be available to learn the concepts. If the teacher is sincere, even if their delivery is poor, the light of knowledge will still be imparted if we remain sincere in learning. Do your part as the student and remember that knowledge is most easily transmitted from the heart of a sincere teacher to the heart of a sincere student.

Another potential burden that Muslim students often face is when studying intersects with the fast of Ramadan. During this month, students have a choice of continuing to fast (potentially risking a loss in productivity) or creating an excuse to skip fasting for the sake of their studies. In these times remember that Allah does not place burdens on us that we are unable to bear. Fasting during studying or taking an exam is not an impossible feat, and studying or taking an exam is not a valid excuse to skip fasting. We need to start with the proper mindset and belief that Allah will not only reward us for our effort, but that He will bless us and make our work easier than perceived. It is a true test of will—a testament to our innate, incredible ability to work when the odds are stacked against us. It will also help us shed bad habits and cultivate a hardworking mentality.

Realistically speaking, however, fasting will likely hurt our productivity; we are only human after all. Instead of lamenting our weakness, we counteract this situation by developing different habits. For example, we can shift studying to either the morning time after *suhoor*[11] or to the few hours prior to or after *iftar*,[12] enabling us to study just after having a meal in the morning or evening and therefore feeling fresh, or just prior to breaking our fast, which would energize us. Although it may not be ideal, we may find our studying is unexpectedly benefited in these times, especially in the early morning hours. This is because the early morning hours are conducive to productivity and are blessed due to the supplication of the Prophet ﷺ, as narrated by the companion Sakhr al-Ghamidi رضي الله عنه that the Prophet ﷺ said:

> *"O Allah, bless my people in their early mornings." When he*
> *sent out a detachment or an army, he sent them at the*
> *beginning of the day. Sakhr was a merchant, and he would*
> *send off his merchandise at the beginning of the day; and he*

---

[11] The meal before dawn consumed prior to the fast.
[12] The meal to break the fast at the time of sunset.

became rich and had much wealth."[13]

Therefore, strive to utilize the early morning to your advantage as it has been blessed by Allah through the answer to a supplication by His Prophet ﷺ. Trust in your ability and trust in the strength that Allah will grant you. Trust in Allah to get you to the goal, even if you think you will feel too hungry or too tired to recognize it. It is not worth skipping the beloved deed of fasting for an exam—no matter how important the latter—because the reward for the former is such that no one knows the extent.[14]

Similarly, be mindful of your privilege to fast as there are others who observe fasting without a plan for *suhoor* or the hope of *iftar*. They do not have a fridge full of food waiting to be consumed; they only hope in the mercy of their Lord to provide for them. It would be a shame for the Muslim student to stand in front of Allah on the Day of Judgment and say that they were too burdened by their studies to fast, when they will be shown examples of people who did fast during their studies and exams as well as examples of people who had less and fasted. It would be a shame then to use an excuse such as "they were stronger than me" when Allah Himself has pronounced that He would not place us in a situation that we could not handle. We should not be so quick to sell our own abilities short. No one can escape from Allah; fasting is better for us, if we only knew.

---

[13] *Sunan Abi Dawud* #2606
[14] *Sahih Muslim* #1151b

Additionally, be mindful that every struggle has a good deed associated with it, no matter how minor it may be. It was narrated by 'A'isha رضي الله عنها that the Prophet ﷺ said:

> *"No calamity befalls a Muslim but that Allah expiates some of his sins because of it, even though it were the prick he receives from a thorn."[15]*

And know that as you become more beloved to Allah, you may be placed under more trials as a means to expiate sins and perhaps increase your rank on the Day of Judgment.[16] No human being would ever want to be burdened or put through trials (even the ones who are close to Allah), it is always better to ask Allah to protect you from trials and to practice the supplications as mentioned in the beginning of the chapter—to plead with Allah not to place a burden on you that you are unable to bear. Therefore, ask Allah to make all of your trials easy for you—including fasting during studying—resting assured that if you are faced with any type of trial, no matter the stakes, you will be able to pass; have faith and proceed forth.

Nevertheless, know that any type of studying is a huge sacrifice. It will test you in the time that you need to be away from family for work and the time it takes to study, and the sheer amount of material to be learned, studied, and mastered will test the limits of your mind. It is an overwhelming but not impossible journey.

---

[15] *Sahih al-Bukhari #5640*
[16] *Jami` at-Tirmidhi #2398*

When any student feels burdened by their courses, they only need to think back to the beautiful verse and promise of Allah, and they will realize that they can deal with their struggles and that theirs are nothing compared to the struggles faced by people around the world. The people of the war-torn lands, our brothers and sisters, bear an unbelievable burden as they are continuously bombarded from all sides and shunned by the rest of the world. Their confidence to live on should be an inspiration to all who seek inspiration, as they are much better than us. Their burden is not like our burden because they are able to handle that burden, and perhaps we are not. Thus, Allah didn't put us through their burden, which shows us that hardships are actually a means of elevating our own potential. In fact, Allah in His perfection uses the Arabic word "*wus*" in the aforementioned verse, which means that He would not order us to do something we are not able to do. But this word has another meaning: "the extent to which we can do something"—in other words, our full potential.[17]

We need to reflect on the burden of studying as Allah encouraging us to reach our full potential as students. Allah gave us a responsibility as privileged students not just to study excellently, but to contribute something more. Allah grants us knowledge, the best school, the best materials, time in which to study, a comfortable home in which to study, and the support of friends and family—and for what? So that we can squander our chance to become leaders in our fields? We should be cognizant that Allah

---

[17] Ustadh Khan, Nouman A. "We Ask Allah. Tafsir of last two verses of Surah Al-Baqarah." March 2015. Youtube Video, 2:07:31. March 2015. https://www.youtube.com/watch?v=Njuq145ESzk

will ask us about what we did with the gifts we were afforded. Did we advance research in the medical field, push our boundaries, and look for new therapies and cures for disease? Did we practice good morals in our businesses and not sell our religion as a commodity? Did we defend the rights of our brothers and sisters when they were wronged, or did we simply look to cash a check? Did we use our creative genius to further the word of Islam in a positive way, perhaps through design and the media? Allah has granted us all a set of strengths, and it is up to us to identify our potential within them; in so doing, our perceived burdens and hardships *become* our potential. They are the sacrifices upon which we build our success, and they become the cherished memories to guide others.

For the student, this means that the burdens of long hours of studying and the extensive amount of coursework that needs to be covered become positive challenges—challenges they know they can overcome. And as the student continually improves their performance, they will undoubtedly realize that they have climbed heights previously perceived as unclimbable. They will realize that their potential could be far greater, and so they are not satisfied with the initial success. They aim even higher and arrive at the realization that not only is there a light at the end of the tunnel for themselves, but that their personal success is also tied to the responsibility of giving back to their community—a community in desperate need of their skill set and expertise.

All of these points revolve around the principle of fostering a positive mindset by implementing the benefit of Islam to our study habits. In this way, our burdens are transformed from sources of grief to sources of motivation, from reasons for procrastination to reasons for working. In time, we are transformed from people who blame to people of reflection, from people demoralized by trials to people yearning to fulfill their potential.

And so we ask Allah to never place on us such a burden that we cannot bear and that He enable us to be cognizant of the amazing ease that accompanies it.

"With the Name of Allah, the Most Merciful, the Most Compassionate

Did We not expand for you, [O Muhammad], your breast?

And We removed from you your burden

Which had weighed upon your back

And raised high for you your repute.

For indeed, with hardship [will be] ease.

Indeed, with hardship [will be] ease.

So when you have finished [your duties], then stand up [for worship].

And to your Lord direct [your] longing."

QUR'AN CHAPTER 94 ("THE RELIEF"): VERSE 1–8

3

A Light at the End of the Tunnel

On the long days and even longer nights during my time as a student, I would often try to look for the light at the end of the tunnel; the flickering light representing the hope at the end of the exam phase and the start of a brief vacation. Studying for finals is an especially difficult time, but it does not last forever, just as organic chemistry, board exams, and academic essays similarly do not last forever. Hard times eventually flow into easy times, but when we constantly focus on the difficult times, we hardly allow ourselves to realize the blessings that we have already been afforded and the good times that await us.

During those difficult periods as a student, I focused on the light instead of the tunnel, developing a habit of imagining myself positively, both during the exam (or other difficult challenge) and immediately afterward. Suffice it to say that most times it turned out okay in my mind's eye and also in reality, building confidence in my ability to tackle different

challenges. Even as a medical resident preparing for difficult patient en-
counters, I visualized myself in my mind's eye in a positive light during
and after the encounter: asking the right questions, getting the right diag-
nosis, building an appropriate treatment plan, and coming out of it in one
piece. In other words, when we visualize our challenges in our mind's eye
ahead of time, we are able to cope with those challenges, even if they don't
turn out the way we positively imagined it. After all, life goes on, this isn't
the last stand.

This exercise may sound comical, but it has a measurable effect on
the psyche that enables a person to maneuver from a position of fear to a
position of confidence. It is similar to the advice given to anyone before a
big game in sports: along with practice, they must imagine themselves taking and making the game-winning shot *before* they can be confident
enough to attempt (and successfully score) the game-winning shot in real
time. Similarly, we must also envision ourselves in a position of success
within our studies.

Many of us are probably familiar with Allah's words when He mentioned:

> *For indeed, with hardship [will be] ease.*
> *Indeed, with hardship [will be] ease.*[18]

Allah revealed these verses to the Prophet ﷺ at a time when he was

---

[18] Qur'an Chapter 94 ("*The Relief*"), verses 5–6

still in the early stages of spreading the message of Islam, and because Islam was a radical change from the status quo—a call for social change and justice within the current system—the ruling elite and even the general population did not take it well. The sarcasm, ridicule, and emotional and physical torture that the Prophet ﷺ and his followers endured when they accepted this new message during the early years was extremely difficult. For example, when the revelation of the Qur'an was withheld for a few nights,[19] the disbelievers even started to mock the Prophet ﷺ and attempted to undermine him by saying that Allah had abandoned him.[20] After all, if Allah loves a person, shouldn't everything in life be easy?

It is at this critical juncture that Allah revealed many verses to ease the heart of the Prophet ﷺ. For example, He revealed *Surah Ad-Duha*[21] and *Surah Ash-Sharh* (quoted in full at the beginning of this chapter), mainly as a consolation for the Prophet ﷺ, but also as a motivational message to keep all the believers moving forward. Allah starts *Surah Ash-Sharh* by asking rhetorical questions to highlight the magnificent blessings that were already bestowed upon the Prophet ﷺ. Indeed, it was Allah who expanded the Prophet's ﷺ chest by putting his mind and his heart at ease by revealing the truth of Islam and giving him purpose, and in so doing removed a heavy burden that had weighed on the Prophet ﷺ. By gifting Islam, Allah honored the Prophet ﷺ with a high station, such that he is

---

[19] The scholars mention that one of the reasons for temporary withholding of the revelation was so that the Prophet ﷺ may long for its return.

[20] *Sahih Muslim* #1797

[21] Qur'an Chapter 93 ("*The Morning Hours*")

often mentioned after the name of Allah and, indeed, even in the *shaha-dah*.[22]

If we reflect on our lives, we will find many instances where Allah has honored us as well. Maybe it was a time when all doors appeared shut and we did not know how we would rise above the challenge, and suddenly a door of opportunity opened from somewhere unexpected. Consider that Allah has already given us the opportunity to study and obtain a decent education with the hopes of entering an honorable profession. It is an honor to be able to read, write, and learn. Therefore, in the instances we feel life is unfair, we should try and be mindful of the people who wish they could be in our place.

After Allah mentions all the blessings conferred upon the Prophet ﷺ, He gives us the truth about life's hardships: that ease accompanies it. He teaches us that whenever we encounter hardship, we should remind our-selves of the positive aspects of our life and the blessings that we already enjoy. In other words, we are to focus on what has been given to us, rather than complain about what He has withheld from us. In this way, our at-tention shifts from emphasizing the present hardship to being grateful for our blessings. This practice is counterintuitive. As humans, we tend to focus on the hardship and its solution, usually paying no attention to what we already have. Allah prescribes the remedy to the stress that builds from this mentality: recognize the hardship but know we can get through it, and that we have not only been given amazing gifts already, but we are also promised more goodness with the hardship.

---

[22] Arabic term meaning "to witness," commonly referred to as the statement of the declaration of faith

In the face of the intense blessings he had been given, the sarcasm and ridicule of his message became a minor inconvenience for the Prophet ﷺ. For the student, the burden of a final exam becomes a temporary problem in a life full of blessings—the blessing of being able to learn and have an opportunity for a career probably being the most relevant. However, it is only natural as the student traverses their path in education—struggling to learn and memorize what they were taught for the semester—that their mind will often wander in worry. They will worry if they will pass while trying to focus on studying, and once the mind is let loose, they will worry about their internship, then landing a respectable job, then being able to get married and support a family. Eventually, worry will consume them until the end of their days. Instead of letting the mind wander to a future over which we have little control, remembering that Allah gave us the opportunity to succeed, the materials from which to study, and the faculty of the senses to be able to learn what is taught, in addition to having the loving support of our family and friends, the sting of finals and studying lessen. Even still, some students may still struggle with adopting this mindset and find themselves unable to deal with their difficult situation.

To address this concern, we must continue with the revelation to understand the next lesson: that sometimes our challenges, problems, and hardships are not necessarily a sign of Allah's displeasure, but a sign of His love. Perhaps they are the means for spiritual purification, to recognize our need for Him, and a means to recognize the gift of amazing ease that accompanies hardships.

The optimism of the verses we have mentioned—that with every hardship there is ease—is palpable through the English translation, but even more fascinating is the fact that the level of optimism is filtered and not as powerful as its Arabic counterpart. As is often the case, the brilliance of Allah's speech is lost in translation. According to the commentary of the verses, Allah mentions that with one hardship (*al-'usr*) there is ease (*yusr*), but not just *ease*—an unlimited amount of ease that would overwhelm the hardship. In the next verse, one would be led to believe that Allah simply repeats Himself to exaggerate the optimistic hope that with hardship is ease (based on the English translation). However, if we study the Arabic deeper, we find that in actuality Allah teaches that *another* ease (*yusr*, as opposed to *al-yusr*[23]) accompanies the *same* hardship (*al-'usr*) already mentioned. In short, Allah is telling us that for every single hardship we encounter it is accompanied by an unlimited amount of ease. What is even more amazing is that when we study the sentence structure that Allah uses in the verse above, we see that He puts the *focus* on the ease, rather than the hardship. Whereas the sentence structure in English gives the impression that the focus (or subject of the sentence) is on the hardship, in Arabic the actual *subject* of the sentence is *ease*.[24] This lends credence to the view that Allah is teaching us to focus on our blessings and ease rather than the hardship (as mentioned earlier).[25]

Some of us may believe that our present hardship has gone on for far

---

[23] The "*Al*" would indicate a specific hardship with a specific ease, but where Allah specified the one hardship, He mentioned two unspecified eases

[24] In Arabic grammar, when the word "*Inna*" (loosely meaning: "indeed") is used, the subject of the sentence becomes the noun that is in the "accusative case" (in Arabic, noted with a special vowel called a "*fatha*," a grammar concept called "*Ism Inna*"). In this verse, the word with the "*fatha*" is "*yusr*" even though it comes at the end of the sentence. Thus, the subject of the verse is ease. See also Footnote 25.

[25] Ustadh Khan, Nouman A. "In Depth Analysis and Tafsir Surah 94 Al-Inshirah." Youtube Video, 1:22:58. Posted April 2011. https://www.youtube.com/watch?v=2BQnt33D6KI

too long, and we may wonder when the ease will come. This is another misunderstanding of the verse above, as the transition word used above (*ma'a*) actually connotes that hardship is *always accompanied* by ease—they come right after the other or together—even if we fail to recognize it. In summary, not only does Allah promise that with every hardship there is amazing ease, He adds that multiple eases come with one hardship. And He repeats the statement out of His love, just as we often repeat statements out of love to assure our loved ones.

Thus, our current hardship and hardships to come become stepping stones to our goals and destinations rather than roadblocks hindering our forward progress. We remind ourselves that at one point in our lives, multiplication and division were the bane of our existence, but now they are the easiest part of the equation. Although each year of school becomes progressively more difficult (in terms of both the amount of learning material and the time spent understanding it), the Muslim student can find solace in the fact that ease arrives with and after all the hardship. We will always have some time off to relax after the tough times during finals, and constantly reinforcing ourselves with this positive attitude can help us overcome any challenge thrown our way.

It is interesting to note that after delivering this message of hope, Allah commands the Prophet ﷺ to stand tall (*fansab*), however, the meaning of "standing tall" has been left open; Allah did not mention a specific deed that qualifies as "*fansab*." For us to apply this verse and follow the Prophet's ﷺ example, we must be proactive in worship in the midst of challenges—for example, by raising our hands in supplication, praying to Allah, or being kind to our parents.

Following this verse, Allah reminds us that our desire should always be to Him.[26] Indeed, the person who has Allah has everything. Let the student rely on Allah and not allow their mood to go through peaks and valleys linked to their hardships. Rather, let them link their happiness to Allah, who provides them blessing upon blessing with each trial that is set before them.

The promise of Allah is true. Envision success and keep moving forward through the dark tunnels, stand tall with patience and prayer, and know that there is a light not only guiding you, but that there will always be a light at the end of every tunnel.

---

[26] Sheikh Qadhi, Yasir. "Khutbah: 'With every difficulty there is ease.'" Filmed Nov. 2012. Youtube Video, 34:50. Posted Nov. 2012. https://www.youtube.com/watch?v=4GVQjh4tI-A

"O you who have believed, seek help through patience and prayer. Indeed, Allah is with the patient."

QUR'AN CHAPTER 2 ("THE COW") VERSE 153

4

Patience and Prayer

Two extremes exist in the spectrum of Muslim students. The first is represented by those who study day and night and overlook the obligations they have toward their Lord; the second is represented by those who increase their worship so much that they neglect their studies and end up struggling with their grades. For us to become successful students, we must seek to find a middle ground between these two extremes.

The ideal Muslim student studies well but does not forget their obligations to their Lord—for example, by committing to prayer on time, even during tough stretches in their studies. Similarly, they do not call upon Allah *only* when they are desperate for His help; rather, they always keep the line of communication open. At the same time, they do not forget that success in school requires their own personal effort through studying, going to class, and reading the required texts, combined with the help of Allah. This hybrid group focuses on excelling not just in school, but also in improving their relationship with Allah through their studies.

Two key ingredients are required to achieve this goal: patience and prayer. However, to be deserving of Allah's help and to achieve success, we must not *just* pray and be patient; rather, we must strive to become *people* of patience and *people* of prayer. While these actions—patience and prayer—naturally increase in tough times, the people of patience and prayer are dedicated to this daily routine in leisure as well.

Our condition during Ramadan perfectly illustrates the phenomenon of actions increasing in tough times for the purpose of building a habit. Ramadan occurs year after year and tests our limits each day with hunger and thirst. We may stand for hours at night while forsaking our sleep and simultaneously juggle both school and work responsibilities. Ramadan teaches us that if we are able to abstain from our carnal *needs* (e.g., food and drink), we can definitely abstain from our *wants*. It enables us to realize our potential and the heights we can climb in a short amount of time, helping us realize that we are able to perform at a high level for the rest of the year. Thus, as we increase our rank in Ramadan, we should leave Ramadan with the same rank and aim to get even better while avoiding falling back to our usual routine.

Studying for school follows a similar design. Finals and midterms can hit us so hard that there are times when we feel that skipping a prayer is the only way to complete the tough coursework and allow us time to recover from lack of sleep. Sometimes, we focus so much on the coursework and studying that we belittle time-tested spiritual tools that can contribute to our success. Unfortunately, even when we do pay attention to these spiritual tools, we often abuse them and implement them incompletely to achieve only worldly ends (such as supplicating to Allah only to pass a class), when in fact there is so much more to be gained than a simple letter grade. Therefore, to achieve success in school, we must change the perception of what it means to pray and be patient. By reexamining these powerful spiritual tools, we will aspire to use them to our advantage—not only to succeed on our exams, but also in the race to Allah.

ON PRAYER

When changing our perception of prayer, we must consider two correlating points: first, we should not sacrifice our time with Allah; second, in doing so, we simultaneously take advantage of our beautiful relationship with Him.

In medical school, I observed many of my colleagues skipping Friday prayers that were offered on campus and organized by their own classmates who were struggling in the same classes. By skipping out on that half hour, some of them did indeed do well in school, but others continued to do the same or worse. Among those who took the time to pray, some did well and some didn't. But the reality is that even if the second group did not do well in school, they were still winners in the sight of Allah, as they did not compromise their obligation to Him for a temporary gain in school. In other words, they understood that sacrificing their time with Allah meant they may potentially enjoy temporary success, but that success would have no blessing and in turn would never be worth it. After all, the temporary challenges that accompany the perceived loss of time (due to obligatory worship) perhaps would have unintended benefits in the long run.

Thus, if we find ourselves so busy that we cannot perform our prayers on time or attend Friday prayers, instead of creating excuses to validate our behavior, we should instead reflect introspectively and reevaluate our study methods. There are people who have much tougher schedules who balance their commitment to Allah with their study time while scoring near the top of the class, doing so with less stress and less overall time for studying. These are the people who do well in their studies and, by the will of Allah, will reap rewards in the Hereafter. To claim that our behavior is necessary because these people are more "intelligent" than us is an unsound conclusion; similarly, instead of being jealous of their perceived "natural talent" and lament our inadequacies, we should heed their example, learn from them, and implement the tools that make them successful.

But can meeting with Allah through prayer really improve our study habits?

This act of meeting with Allah—five times a day every day for the rest of our lives—in and of itself is a manifestation of our love for Allah and His love for us. Consider that every injunction sent by Allah was sent *down* upon mankind through the Prophet ﷺ, but Allah brought the Prophet ﷺ *up* to Himself to receive the injunction of prayer. It is this gift from Allah—prayer—that the Prophet ﷺ relied upon in times of distress and in times of ease. Prayer is the tool that the Prophet ﷺ used to escape the daily grind of life, as he is reported to have said,

"Oh Bilal, call iqamah²⁷ for prayer: give us comfort by it."²⁸

The Prophet ﷺ understood that prayer was direct communication with Allah without the need for intermediaries; he showed proper respect, knowing that if he asked the Most Generous, he would not leave empty-handed.

How is it possible for the Prophet ﷺ to consider prayer as *comfort* when many of us sometimes view prayer as a burden that gets in the way of "important," time-sensitive tasks or as an inconvenience at work or school? The answer lies in the attitude of the Prophet ﷺ toward prayer. He did not treat it as a troublesome interruption because he knew its value. He knew that as soon as he lifted his hands and started to recite, he had a direct connection with the Master, the Provider, the Capable. It comforted him to be in the spiritual presence of the One who can fulfill his needs and lift the stressors of worldly life. He prayed as if he could see Allah, and though he could not, he was aware that Allah could see him. It was a treasured spiritual experience, not just an exercise of ritual, and he took his time to communicate—especially with *Surah Al-Fatiha* (Chapter 1 of the Qur'an and a required part of prayer)—because it was not an afterthought but rather the *essence* of the conversation.

Therefore, we should not rush to get the prayer over with. We must strive to take our time and enjoy the pleasant conversation with Allah, His acknowledgement of our praise, and His granting of our wishes.²⁹ Even taking our time, it would surely take no more than five to ten minutes,

---

²⁷ The second and final call to prayer just before the beginning of an obligatory prayer
²⁸ *Sunan Abi Dawud #4985*
²⁹ *Sahih Muslim #395*

enough to fit into any busy schedule and definitely not enough time to adversely affect our studies. Therefore, trust your time with Allah and re-learn the value of five good minutes.

When we commit to becoming people of prayer—by not just performing prayer but *establishing* it as part of our daily routine—we find that many of our perceived hardships become easier. If we set time for Allah, do we really think He will forsake us in our time of need? Do we really think He won't help us when calculus seems like a foreign language? Are we really going to fail when we "lose" time by praying on time? Whether we pray, drive an extra fifteen minutes to attend Friday prayer, or read a page of the Qur'an for fifteen minutes before bedtime, we give that time—out of the limited time that we have—to Allah. Be confident that it was a profitable investment. The return will manifest itself in blessings that we can only begin to imagine. The time that we give to Allah will be transformed into a blessing (perhaps, for example, making a lecture easier to understand).

For a person of prayer, what would have taken four hours to comprehend takes two instead, because there is *blessing* in their time. A person committed to prayer understands that if there are 100 slides left in their lecture for review—slides that make absolutely no sense to them and with only a few days left until the big exam—instead of complaining about the situation, they proactively take five minutes to perform two units of prayer, comforting themselves by remembering Allah's help and having the confidence that these actions will get their work done. They know that as long as they are a person of prayer, they are *inshaAllah*, deserving of the help of Allah—and a powerful help that is.

To continue, when we commit to our prayers, we realize that the prayers and their times allow for a natural propensity toward managing time effectively in a divinely ordained schedule. Glory be to Allah for His wisdom in all things.

It is well known that sleeping too little and sleeping too much are detrimental and not only lead to an unhealthy lifestyle, but that they also impair proper consolidation of learning (see Chapter 8). In His wisdom, Allah created the night as a means to rest for the day ahead, but He ordained *fajr*[30] which requires us to rise when most everyone else is still asleep. When a person of prayer performs *fajr*, then commits to further acts of worship before transitioning to their studies, they will find enumerable blessings and ease.[31] We may complain that we are too tired or that it is too difficult to wake up for this prayer. When afflicted with this thought, we need to ask ourselves, "Would it be difficult to wake up for an early flight? To work out in the gym? To watch our favorite TV show?" We all have priorities, but many times prayer is not one of them. Consider the people who walk their pets early *every* morning; they have no incentive to do this except for their love for their pet and their desire to be fit. We should be ashamed if we do not feel the same love to meet and speak with Allah. If we commit to waking up for *fajr*, we will not only reap the reward that Allah has promised in the next life, but the habit of prayer will help us refocus our mind and set the tone for the rest of the day studying.

Imagine waking up, purifying yourself, performing *fajr*, and *then* starting your day by studying. Consider the extra two hours gained before

---

[30] The morning prayer, performed between dawn and sunrise.
[31] See footnote 13.

school begins and the amount of work you could get done beforehand, such as reviewing past lectures or previewing upcoming lectures. Without spiritual fuel, our engines start to sputter, and so, instead of focusing on the study material, our minds drift and we create excuses and become unhappy with our condition. There will be times where our prayer is not perfect, but if we commit to it every morning despite our struggle with it, we will be in a position to fine tune the *fajr* prayer, helping to build a more efficient morning routine that will illuminate the rest of the day.

Before proceeding, it is worth noting that prayer in congregation is an extremely important part of our religion, and a means of multiplying the reward for prayer, up to twenty-seven degrees compared to offering it alone.[32] Islam stresses the importance of community, and one way to embrace the rest of the community is to regularly pray in congregation, even if it is with just one other person. To expand further, it is highly encouraged to attend prayers in the mosque as much as possible because that will amplify the reward, especially since the congregation is typically larger. Allah has prescribed prayer at appointed times, and one of the benefits of adhering to them is that it allows the Muslim to continue the spiritual high throughout the day, reminding us of our connection with Allah; sharing this worship with others only helps motivate us communally and keeps us together on a spiritual high. Of the congregational prayers, one cannot overstate the importance of the congregational prayers for *fajr*, as it sets the mood for the day. If you are skeptical, try it for a few days and observe the change it breathes into your life. Further, if one commits to

---

[32] *Sahih al-Bukhari #645*

fajr and *isha*[33] in congregation, it is as if they prayed the entire night![34]

Even having started the day with *fajr*, as the day progresses we inevitably get lost in the pursuit of this world and the advancement of our studies. Allah ordained two prayers during the day as a break from the world and a chance to refocus. When we take the time to actively seek these prayers—*dhuhr*[35] and '*asr*[36]—from our busy schedules, we carve out a section of our life where we are not dictated by the waves of the world and instead reconnect with our Master, reminding ourselves of the common truths that will carry us through the rest of the day (for example, that our life and work are for Allah, which helps to purify our intention). A second truth is that the burden of our study is within our scope, the acknowledgment of which allows us to ask for help when we feel we are drowning and to use the prayer as our life vest. And there are many other truths, many of which we will mention later (including thankfulness, reliance on Allah, and building up habits slowly). Thus, the prayer becomes a safe haven in the hurricane of a busy day.

As we return from school or after a hard day's work, day descends into night, and we meet with Allah in the *maghrib*[37] prayer. *Maghrib* allows us to reflect on the day that has passed, on the beneficial things we did and the sins for which we need to repent, all while looking to what we have prepared for tomorrow. Finally, as the night sky dominates and we get ready for sleep, we close the book on the day by pausing to complete

---

[33] The late evening prayer.

[34] *Sahih Muslim* #656

[35] Prayer performed in the afternoon right after the sun moves away from its zenith.

[36] Late afternoon prayer performed after *dhuhr* and before sunset.

[37] Prayer that is performed right after sunset.

'isha before we sleep, remembering to rely upon Allah to help us remember what we have studied. Thus, we complete the cycle of the remembrance of Allah as the last deed before we sleep and the first deed when we wake. How can Allah forsake His slave that sincerely remembers, worships, and calls upon Him in the action which He loves most?

> *But what if our schedule does not fit with the divinely*
> *ordained prayer schedule?*

Sometimes in our forgetfulness we may oversleep for *fajr* or we may miss a prayer due to some hardship. In these instances, we must first never lose hope, as it is forbidden to despair in the mercy of Allah.[38] After we realize this, we seek forgiveness, repent, and resolve to take action to never allow ourselves to miss prayer again. Lastly, in that instant that we remembered we forgot the prayer, we must leave whatever we are doing and complete the missed prayer to make up for it.[39]

As for those who intentionally miss prayer in order to study, they should reflect that studying is not a valid excuse to miss the prayer. Know that whether we like it or not, whether we believe it will happen or not, we *will* bear witness to what we have done in this world in front of Allah. Those who skip their prayers in favor of more time studying already bear witness to their sin as they have colleagues beside them who used to pray while having the same responsibilities in this world.

Instead of turning away further, we should try our best to begin to

---

[38] Qur'an Chapter 39 (*"The Troops"*), verse 53
[39] *Sahih Muslim* #684

implement the prayer in our lives as much as we are able. If we do this, we will slowly find that the fruit of our labor in this world will be less exhausting to collect. Some of us may miss prayer but have the moral sense to make it up later, and while this is commendable in the sense that we do not leave it off completely, we must strive to be better and perform it on time. Just as it is impractical to skip breakfast and lunch and combine it with dinner all at once at the end of the day, so too is it inappropriate to skip all the prayers and combine them all at once when we have a free moment.

What of the person who stays up all night because they had no other time to study before that? Firstly, it is never advisable to "pull an all-nighter" to study, but to give this advice without admitting that I am guilty of this would be hypocritical. We will, in our naïveté as young students, find ourselves at some point forsaking sleep during the night to study or complete a project. My advice in this situation is to follow the special people who have made it their habit to pray *tahajjud*[40] in addition to the daily prayers. These are the people who voluntarily meet with Allah in the dead of night, enabling them to advance even further.

Practically speaking, it would be more beneficial for us to pray at least two units of extra prayer sometime in our studies during an all-nighter than to completely ignore the power of those two units. Similarly, if we find ourselves staying up late most nights, then it would be better to sleep after adding at least two units of prayer than to sleep without them at all. Be mindful of the special spiritual means of the night prayer as an extremely

---

[40] Voluntary prayers performed at night between *isha* and *fajr*.

reliable method of helping us toward our goals. It is narrated by Abu Hurairah رضي الله عنه that the Prophet ﷺ said:

> *"Our Lord, the Blessed, the Superior, comes every night down on the nearest Heaven to us when the last third of the night remains, saying: 'Is there anyone to invoke Me, so that I may respond to invocation? Is there anyone to ask Me, so that I may grant him his request? Is there anyone seeking My forgiveness, so that I may forgive him?'"*[41]

Know then that Allah asks if *anyone* is in need so that He may grant it, in the last one-third of the night, *every night.* Thus, if the Muslim student is *desperate* for anything, such as the help of Allah in their studies, then waking up (or interrupting their study during an all-nighter) in the middle of the night for prayer to plead for Allah's help becomes a wise strategy. A practical way of implementing this practice if one sleeps at an appropriate time is to wake up thirty minutes prior to the start of *fajr* and perform a few extra units of prayer and to increase in *dua'* during this beautiful time. We ask Allah to make us among the people who take advantage of the doors that He opens.

A final possibility for disrupting the schedule of the daily prayers is if someone works the night shift. This is a difficult shift not only because of the stress of working at night and the disruption of our natural circadian rhythm, but also because of the stress of finding time to sleep during the

---

[41] *Sahih al-Bukhari* #1145

day while maintaining the daily prayers (especially when prayers are close together in timing).

My advice from personal experience is to first try to implement at least two units of prayer as described above during the night shift, though sometimes this is not possible. Secondly and more importantly, the only feasible way to overcome this challenge during the day is to organize sleep around the prayers. Although it is difficult, trying to find a block of sleep in between prayers is better than sleeping and waking up whenever we like, a choice that carries with it the potential of missed prayers.

For example, one could sleep after their shift and up until a half hour before *asr* time or perhaps between the beginning of *dhuhr* time and the end of *asr* time. After all, if we had an important meeting for work with our boss at a certain time, even if it was after a night shift, we would set multiple alarms in a staggering fashion or make sure to delegate someone to wake us up. We should undertake the same care with our meetings with the Master of the Universe.

Similarly, I would advise that each person honestly assess their need for sleep. For example, some people are adept at taking naps and can take a second nap even after waking from the first one. It would be easier for these people to wake up for *dhuhr* and *asr* at their appointed times and then return to sleep twice. For people like myself who find it difficult to sleep after waking the first time, it is better to sleep in a block of time in between prayers and get about five to six hours of sleep, if possible, in that block, and make up for the lost sleep later.[42]

---

[42] Note there may be an extreme circumstance in which someone may have a legitimate excuse to combine prayers, but this would need to be discussed with a qualified scholar who looks into a

Lastly, before ending our present discussion regarding becoming people of prayer, we must also mention the Friday prayer and the importance
of voluntary prayers. No matter our circumstance, we must always make
our best effort to attend Friday prayer. Not only is it an obligation, but it
will grant further blessings to our work. If you are not able to attend it in
a mosque, then at least try to set up a time where a few Muslims who work
or study with you can meet for the Friday prayer and perform a shorter
version amongst yourselves. The key is for us to perform it and put forth
our best efforts. Remembering Allah within our work and making the sacrifice to remember Him by attending Friday prayer is a means to success.
Therefore, do not run away from Allah. He is the best provider and will
grant us what is better for us if only we recognize it.[43]

As for the voluntary prayers, amongst many of us is a toxic notion
that we can simply ignore them because they are "just sunnah." Once the
intelligent student is able to commit themselves to pray the obligatory
prayers on time, they will not be satisfied. This is because they will see
tangible results with this first step to Allah, and because they want more
success, they will take a few more minutes to connect with Allah in the
form of the voluntary units of prayer associated with the obligatory prayers. Those who commit to the voluntary prayers will be successful in this
world and will be busy investing in properties in Paradise,[44] but the reward
for these prayers goes beyond even that. The student who commits to
these prayers will continue to elevate their relationship with Allah, and no

person's specific circumstances.
[43] Qur'an Chapter 62 ("*The Friday Congregation*"), verses 9–11
[44] *Jami` at-Tirmidhi* #415 and also *Sahih Muslim* #728

one can hinder a person from achieving anything if Allah is with them. Reflect on the power of these people in the following narration, on the authority of Abu Hurairah رضي الله عنه who said the Prophet ﷺ said:

"Allah said, 'I will declare war against him who shows hostility to a pious worshipper of Mine. And the most beloved things with which My slave comes nearer to Me, are the religious obligations I have enjoined upon him; and My slave keeps on coming closer to Me through performing extra deeds till I love him. When I love him I become his sense of hearing with which he hears, and his sense of sight with which he sees, and his hand with which he grips, and his leg with which he walks; and if he asks Me, I will give him, and if he asks My protection, I will protect him; and I do not hesitate to do anything as I hesitate to take the soul of the believer, for he hates death, and I hate to disappoint him.'"[45]

In conclusion, once a person of prayer adheres to the divinely ordained schedule for the daily prayers, they realize that every block in between a prayer is an opportunity for work or for leisure.

Choosing to devote ourselves to perfect the craft we pursue through studying—from the moment we wake as well as during these blocks of time—is the essence of discipline. When we interrupt our studies for a few minutes for the prayer, we remind ourselves that Allah is the best helper,

---

[45] *Sahih al-Bukhari #6502*

building discipline within us and granting us motivation to push through our current tasks. Hidden beneath these realizations is the fact that as we commit to establishing prayer, we are unconsciously building a discipline that will allow ourselves to look past the temporary discomfort of reading five pages from the required reading, reviewing last week's lecture, or preparing for a presentation. We will realize that, along with the prayer, we have unknowingly developed patience, which enables us to study more efficiently and more deeply than we ever imagined.

ON PATIENCE

Everything we want to achieve in our life requires patience, and although some of us are naturally inclined toward patience, most of us need to practice and fail many times to truly practice it. Consider course material that has been presented over the past three weeks: you can cover it in a day, but you will not master it until you put a concerted effort in place to learn the material patiently over time. Take the time and exercise patience to learn the material as it is taught to you so that it is less stressful in the end. Understand that it will take multiple reviews to fully master the material, and that although exams may appear to be easy for the smartest people in the class, they too also commit to meticulous, patient review of the subject matter. Patience is to understand that although we sacrifice our leisure time in the present moment, we are investing in a career that will be fruitful and give us blessings in this world and the Hereafter.

The more we struggle with patience, the higher the reward will be. Know that Allah notices when we are patiently wading through pages and pages of work, even though we feel like slamming the textbook into the wall. Know that Allah notices when we patiently go through the required prerequisite courses that seem so frivolous to our career goals. And know that Allah notices the tough days and the thoughts of quitting that cross our mind. Erase those negative thoughts and keep moving forward! No problem in life is permanent; as the old adage goes, this too shall pass.

Patience is a virtue that we must continuously work upon, fine-tune, and nurture. We need patience when we are stuck in a traffic jam or in the longest line in the supermarket, when we are holding back the easy reactions and replacing them with difficult reactions that take patience. During these moments it is important to realign, take a deep breath, and focus on the good of the moment. Perhaps the traffic jam will allow more time for introspection and self-discovery, and the line at the supermarket a time to review what we have memorized for class. The student can specifically practice building this virtue with their studies and their prayers; by committing to discipline in these actions, they will find their patience for everything steadily improving. Patience is a gift from Allah, a far-reaching, amazing gift given to the people who practice and *want* to be patient.[46]

So instead of impatiently asking, "When will Allah help me?" think instead, "Would Allah, in His infinite mercy, allow me to fail if I sacrificed my study time for His sake? Would He not see that and compensate me?" And after these reflections, patiently ask, "Oh Allah, please help me to be patient."

---

[46] *Sunan an-Nasai* #2588

The importance of patience cannot be overstated. It is a comprehensive gift, but on top of the gift of having patience, the greater gift is that Allah is *with* the people of patience, as He says:

> *"O you who have believed, seek help through patience and prayer. Indeed, Allah is with the patient."*[47]

What better assistance could a person ask for than the help of Allah?

In summary, to be on the path of studying from the Islamic approach, we commit ourselves to becoming people of prayer and patience. We commit to connecting with Allah multiple times a day to confess our weaknesses and seek His aid, day in and day out, until the day we return to Him. Therefore, we should be mindful of what we say and what we ask during our prayer, being sure that Allah knows, listens, and responds.

---

[47] Qur'an Chapter 2 ("*The Cow*"), verse 153. Note there are many other verses in the Qur'an that indicate that Allah is with the people who practice patience

And when My servants ask you, [O Muhammad], concerning Me—indeed I am near. I respond to the invocation of the supplicant when he calls upon Me. So let them respond to Me [by obedience] and believe in Me that they may be [rightly] guided.

QUR'AN CHAPTER 2 ("THE COW") VERSE 186

5

An Answered Supplication

In 2014, Chapman University reported that the greatest fear in America (25 percent of those polled) was the fear of public speaking. Many of us likely have the same fear, manifested, for example, in getting up in front of an audience to deliver a speech only to fail so miserably that everyone laughs. However, as with many perceived fears we deal with in life, the fear of public speaking and the possibility of failure are mostly overblown. With time, effort, patience, and practice, this fear will slowly fade away, elevating even those who struggle with public speaking to eloquently command the stage in such a way that one may think they were born with the innate talent to captivate an audience.

There are many reasons a person may fear public speaking. They may not be eloquent in speech, may sound robotic, may make a mistake in content while speaking to a panel of experts, or may have an incorrect understanding of a concept. To address these fears, we usually carefully craft and proofread our speeches and practice for hours to make sure our delivery is sound, free of mistakes, rooted in correct understanding, and as eloquent as possible.

While we practice and care for the larger audience, there is an audience that many of us think little of in terms of preparation and are even less nervous about. How much have we truly reflected on the Majesty of Allah, every moment of our lives that we have requested something of Him, in other words, made *dua*[48]? Imagine medieval messengers walking into the royal palaces and addressing the heads of empires: think about how much they must have prepared, how sweaty their palms used to be, and how afraid they were to address their audience. Even in present times, when we request something of a person of a certain authority, we take care to dress our best and speak with a respectful tone and clear speech to maximize our chances of obtaining our request. But when it comes to Allah, many of us either ask too little, too late, or impatiently while relying on an unprepared request devoid of sincerity, class, and respect for authority.

Many people engage in an extreme amount of *dua'* when they are desperate, as a last-ditch effort to substitute for their lack of effort (e.g., right before exams, expecting Allah to deliver a good result without studying), or their requests are devoid of sincerity (e.g., expecting Allah to have a tailor-made *dua'* for their specific need). We even go as far as becoming more attentive to religious obligations and duties in our times of extreme need, all in a selfish effort to obtain good grades, which is actually very common human behavior.

---

[48] Arabic term meaning "to supplicate or request of Allah," a concept that will be expanded upon in this chapter

As we face struggles in life and are at the edge of desperation, we are forced to reexamine our outlook on the world and slowly (or sometimes rapidly) return to our *fitrah*[49] as we dramatically appeal to a Higher Power for help. An example of this behavior in the Qur'an is when Allah vividly describes Pharaoh's last moments (at the time of Prophet Moses عليه السلام) when he was at the point of imminent death. It was only then he realized the truth and the error of his ways that he became desperate to believe in Allah to save his life, but at that point it was too late. So too, many who disbelieve in Allah also rely on Him when they experience some disaster, as Allah mentions:

> *It is He who enables you to travel on land and sea until,*
> *when you are in ships and they sail with them by a good*
> *wind and they rejoice therein, there comes a storm wind*
> *and the waves come upon them from everywhere and they*
> *assume that they are surrounded, supplicating Allah,*
> *sincere to Him in religion, "If You should save us from this,*
> *we will surely be among the thankful."*[50]

Therefore, we should be careful not to adopt a selective approach of only calling upon Allah in times of desperation. Be consistent in your calling; do not just pick up the phone when you are going through challenges, but continue to call upon Him in times of ease.

---

[49] Arabic term defined as "the way a person is created, with his original and pure state of being." Dr. Imad Bayoun. *Belief and the Human Mind* (Cedar Graphis, 2016), 13-14

[50] Qur'an Chapter 10 ("*Jonah*"), verse 22

Dua' is probably the most well-known and oft-used tool in the arsenal of the Muslim student. Because of this, it is essential to learn about it and use it appropriately. Just like in public speaking, our ability to make *dua'* effectively in front of the audience—in this case Allah—relies heavily on our ability to carefully craft an effective *dua'* by using etiquette taught by the Prophet ﷺ, while being sincere in our request. Each student should assess their ability to make *dua'*—how effective it is and how frequently it is made—just as they prepare for their projects or before a public presentation.

To perform effective *dua'*, we must first learn its significance in the religion. *Dua'* is referred to as worship, as stated in the famous hadith, narrated by Al-Nuʿman ibn Basheer رضي الله عنهم who heard the Prophet ﷺ say:

"Supplication is worship."[51]

Dua' is referred to as worship for many reasons, but probably chief among these is the fact that the one engaging in *dua'* humbles themselves and submits to the Giver to answer their request. Relying exclusively on Allah leads to humility; although we may think we are able to accomplish our tasks on our own, we realize that, inevitably, they will not be accomplished without His help. In other words, the task can be completed by either asking Allah's help or not, but the one who ignores Allah will not reap the blessing and will be deprived of the chance to worship Him in

---

[51] *Sunan Abi Dawud* #1479 and others

this capacity.

Regarding this last statement, a person may ask: then what is the point of asking Allah if the task is completed by many people who do not worship Allah?

The answer lies—at its core—in belief. If we had true belief and relied on Allah to help us with our tasks, we would not have a reason *not* to ask Him. We would pity the one who did not take the chance to get closer to their Lord by requesting His help in even the most mundane worldly affairs. The one who asks Allah is certain that He will help them, and so is relieved as they put their burden in the hands of Allah and surrenders to His will. The one who feels helpless and as though they cannot do anything can make *dua'*. These are the people who are able to hope when others feel hopeless. They have the foresight that the world and its bounties are not the end of the story and that the ending will be revealed on the Day of Judgment. In other words, they know that the true blessing is not in the material gain of this world, but extends to the Hereafter, in Paradise, with abundant rewards.

Beyond the blessing of asking Allah's help is that He *guided* us to ask for His help. Once we can separate the blessing of the material world from the blessing of being able to worship Allah—that the two are not equal in profit—we will start to actualize our belief. These students are the successful ones who seek to find reasons to excel in their worship of Allah while excelling in their studies. After all, what an excellent, easy way to excel in worship via engaging in persistent *dua*! And Allah is the greatest ally anyone could ever ask for.

The amazing aspect of *dua'* in the Islamic tradition is that it implies the majesty of Allah and His mercy on His slaves. Consider that Allah places no intermediaries between Him and us, His *slaves*. Even in our imperfect, sinful, miniscule states, we are encouraged to ask and request of Allah *directly*. Reflect on His power to listen and to grant—to any one of us out of the billions of humans who live today and who have lived before us and who will come after us. As Allah says:

> *"And when My servants ask you, [O Muhammad],*
> *concerning Me—indeed I am near. I respond to the*
> *invocation of the supplicant when he calls upon Me. So let*
> *them respond to Me [by obedience] and believe in Me that*
> *they may be [rightly] guided."*[52]

An incredible point to consider from the verse is that Allah does not instruct the Prophet ﷺ to "tell" the people the answer about Allah; rather, He *Himself* answers the question to the one who asks, directly and personally. Indeed, He *is* near and He answers, whenever we call upon Him. It then behooves us as His slaves to respond to His call, to answer it to the best of our ability, and to believe in Him to attain true guidance. What a magnificent relationship the believer has with their Lord, and what an opportunity for those who seek success!

Before continuing to the etiquette of effective *dua'*, it is worth noting certain times in which *dua'* is readily accepted (e.g., when a person is

---

[52] Qur'an Chapter 2 ("*The Cow*"), verse 186

breaking their fast,[53] traveling,[54] making *dua'* in the time between the *ad-han*[55] and the *iqamah*,[56] an hour on Friday,[57] during rain,[58] and in the last hours of the night[59]). Another time to increase *dua'* is in prostration. When we put our face on the ground, we acknowledge that we are helpless in front of Allah, the Most High. Abu Hurairah رضي الله عنه narrates that the Prophet ﷺ is reported to have said:

> *"The closest that any one of you may be to his Lord is when he is prostrating, so increase your supplications then."*[60]

For this reason, it is imperative that we increase our *dua'* during prostration in addition to *dua'* we make in general (i.e., even during the prostration in our obligatory prayers, after the prescribed sayings).[61] Thus, making *dua'* in prostration not only provides an opportunity for us to seek the help of Allah, but it also affords us the chance to improve our patience and concentration during our prayer.

Another simple, effective way to succeed is to enlist the help of our parents. The care our mothers and fathers have taken for us to succeed manifests itself in many ways, sometimes obvious and sometimes hidden

---

[53] Al-Bayhaqi; see *Saheeh al-Jaami'*, 2032; *al-Saheehah*, 1797 (https://islamqa.info/en/22438)

[54] Ibid.

[55] Arabic word for the call to prayer.

[56] *Jami` at-Tirmidhi* #212

[57] *Sahih Muslim* #852

[58] *Sunan Abi Dawud* #2540

[59] See footnote 41.

[60] *Sahih Muslim* #482

[61] Note there is a difference of opinion regarding the language in which supplication can be made during prostration. The reader is encouraged to seek the advice of their local religious leader regarding this matter.

(For example, they may never reveal the toil of hard labor they endured to finance our studies). We would do well to remember their effort and sacrifice for our sake during times when we think they are hard on us, as they encourage us to be the best. To help ourselves, we should ask our parents to make *dua'* for us to succeed.[62] Not only will this lead to tangible results in our studies, but it will also, at the same time, nurture a healthier relationship with our parents. This is because we sought their help in an important part of our life—which they will appreciate—and when we benefit from the results, we will appreciate their contribution to our lives even more.

Taking all of this into consideration, it should come as no surprise that when we find ourselves studying while fasting, instead of lamenting that we are not able to put more time into studying, we should adjust by studying as much as we are physically able and commit to making an increased amount of *dua'* for our exam (and also for good things in general) in hopes that our fasting would be a means to an accepted *dua'*. Similarly, if we are unexpectedly traveling during finals, we can reflect on traveling as a blessing instead of a hurdle because it is a means to increase in *dua'* when we are not able to study. And as mentioned in the previous chapter, we can also take advantage of those last precious hours of the night tawakkul to pray and make *dua'* (preferably both, but whatever we are able to do), especially if we find ourselves in the middle of an all-nighter.

---

[62] *Sunan Ibn Majah* #3862

HOW DO WE SPEAK TO OUR LORD?

The Prophet ﷺ practiced certain etiquette of *dua'*, which were later explained by the early generations of scholars. These practices are essentially the tools that allow us to carefully craft effective *dua'* that are purposeful, meaningful, and worship that Allah loves. The first prerequisite, of course, is to ask Allah exclusively and with sincerity. A few other practices are listed below, in no particular order (though none are absolutely required, they are delineated from the practice of the Prophet ﷺ) for the benefit of the author and reader:

To be in a state of purity[63]

Although one can make *dua'* at any time and in any state, Allah loves those who purify themselves, and as we purify ourselves before praying and reading the Qur'an, it is important to try to be in a state of cleanliness when requesting help from Allah.

To face the direction of the Ka'bah[64]

To face the same direction when we pray is an action the Prophet ﷺ is reported to have done while making *dua'* at different points in his life (for example, before the Battle of Badr). It is also a symbolic gesture of taking heed of a unified direction of worship, helping us to further focus our attention and be mindful in our request.

To raise our hands and look down

As the Prophet ﷺ mentioned in the hadith, Allah feels ashamed to let

---

[63] *Sahih al-Bukhari* #4323
[64] *Sahih Muslim* #1763

any hand remain empty when it is raised up to Him.[65] Additionally, looking down while making *dua'* is an act of humility and helps us maintain our focus on Allah, preventing potential distractions. This may be easier to understand when we compare how we interact with dignitaries and certain people of esteem, as many times we unknowingly ask out of humbleness by bowing our head; to Allah, however, is the best example.

To start by praising Allah and to ask by His names

As Allah says:

> *"And to Allah belong the best names, so invoke Him by*
> *them. And leave [the company of] those who practice*
> *deviation concerning His names. They will be recompensed*
> *for what they have been doing."*[66]

Normally when we ask someone for something, we recognize their positive qualities or the qualities that will allow them to fulfill our request. For example, we recognize the surgeon and their ability to perform procedures (and perhaps their reputation as a good physician) and trust that they will be able to perform the surgery competently, excellently, and with a low risk for complications. Similarly, when we start to make *dua'*, we should also remember to praise Allah for the many bounties He has already given to us and call upon Him by His beautiful names. This encourages us to be people of thanks and raises our confidence that He will help us. Allah Himself teaches us this formula in the opening of the

---

[65] *Sunan Abi Dawud* #1488
[66] Qur'an Chapter 7 (*"The Heights"*), verse 180

Qur'an, as He starts with praise and recognition of His mercy and His authority over the Day of Judgment and our reliance on Him, and then after that teaches us to ask for guidance to the straight path.

To send peace and blessings on the Prophet ﷺ

One of the greatest means by which *dua'* is answered is to send peace and blessings upon the Prophet ﷺ. When we mention the one whom Allah loves, we put ourselves in a better position to ask. Imagine if we were in a state of great need, and instead of asking for help with that need first, we chose to send peace and blessings upon the Prophet ﷺ. In other words, we prefer he whom Allah loves above our very own urgent needs. How could Allah possibly let us down when we start with this touching gesture? Following this practice, it is recommended that, after starting *dua'* with the praise of Allah, we next send peace and blessings upon the Prophet ﷺ.[67] Following this, we can mention our needs. And when we run out of requests or don't know what else to say, we can always extend the conversation with Allah and increase our rank by asking Him to send peace and blessings upon the Prophet ﷺ.[68]

To make dua' in secret, unless we are leading a group dua'
As Allah says:

> *"Call upon your Lord in humility and privately; indeed,*
> *He does not like transgressors."*[69]

---

[67] *Sunan Abi Dawud* #1481 and *Jami` at-Tirmidhi* #3477
[68] *Sahih Muslim* #408
[69] Qur'an Chapter 7 ("*The Heights*"), verse 55

Expressing our need to Allah in secret and not relying on anyone else helps improve our sincerity, while also perhaps protecting us from showing off our religiosity.

To ask for yourself first, then others

We should take care of our needs first, then ask Allah to help others. This is the Prophetic formula; for example, when Prophet Abraham عليه السلام made supplication, he included himself first and then his offspring and his parents.[70]

To repeat dua' three times[71]

When we persistently ask others for something, repeating our requests many times or daily, more often than not our persistence will annoy the requested party. By contrast, Allah loves it when we go back to Him constantly. With Allah, insistence is the *rule* and not the exception. Allah loves that we continuously knock on the door and ask Him, so we should show urgency in our need and persist in asking.

To not say "inshaAllah"[72]

We should be firm and equip ourselves with the expectation that our *dua'* will be answered. We should not feel that we burden Allah with *any* request, as any request is miniscule in comparison with His majesty. Reflect on the power of Allah as the Giver in the following narration:

> "*O My servants, even if the first amongst you and the last amongst you and the whole human race of yours and that of*

---

[70] Qur'an Chapter 14 ("*Abraham*"), verses 35–41
[71] *Jami` at-Tirmidhi* #2572
[72] *Sahih al-Bukhari* #6339

jinns also all stand in one plain ground and you ask Me and I
confer upon every person what he asks for, it would not in any
way, cause any loss to Me (even less) than that which is caused
to the ocean by dipping the needle in it."[73]

To ask for the best possible outcome

Sometimes we receive only what we ask for, often leaving wonderful opportunities or potential bonuses on the table because we feared asking too much. As a result of feeling too sinful or thinking about all our shortcomings, we sometimes feel shy about asking Allah for something we think we don't deserve. In spite of those feelings, don't let *shaytan*[74] trick you into closing the line of communication with Allah. Indeed, Allah even answered shaytan's request for his punishment to be postponed until the Day of Judgment,[75] and none of us is worse than shaytan.

Instead of feeling shy, we should ask Allah for the best, no matter our current situation. After all, He is the most generous, and nothing is too great in His sight. One has nothing to lose by asking Allah; we only lose if we shut the door that Allah left open for us. Therefore, ask Allah plentifully and for the best possible outcome, just as the Prophet ﷺ recommended when he instructed his companions to ask for the best and highest level of Paradise.[76]

To not ask for harmful things

To ask for the impossible means we fail to realize our current form as

---

[73] *Sahih Muslim #2577*
[74] The Arabic equivalent for Satan, the devil.
[75] Qur'an Chapter 7 ("*The Heights*"), verses 14–15
[76] *Sahih al-Bukhari 2790*

imperfect human beings. Nature and its laws only bend when Allah allows it and for a specific purpose, such as the parting of the sea for Prophet Moses عليه السلام and the virgin birth of Prophet Jesus عليه السلام. In addition, we should avoid asking Allah to punish us,[77] as Allah's mercy is greater than any sin we have committed. Lastly, in general we should avoid making *dua'* against others (there are some exceptions to the rule, which are beyond the scope of this book). A practical example for our purposes is this: do not ask Allah to have another student in the class fail, because it is not within a Muslim's character to wish harm upon others, especially fellow Muslims.

To make dua' as comprehensive as possible

The best, most comprehensive *dua'* anyone can learn are from the Qur'an and the sunnah. Sometimes we may be in a rush or we may focus on a single specific request (e.g., to pass an exam), but more than that we should always try to add—in addition to a specific request—a general request to be on the path of righteousness, as well as for the reward in the Hereafter and for protection from punishment in the Hereafter. Developing this habit will enable us to remember our purpose and refocus our intention as we delve deeper into studies. An example of a simple yet comprehensive *dua'* to commit to memory and use when trying to increase in knowledge is this:

"… My Lord, increase me in knowledge."[78]

[77] *Sahih Muslim* #2688
[78] Qur'an Chapter 20 ("*Taha*"), part of verse 114 (Transliteration: *Rabbi Zidnee 'Ilma*)

To say "Ameen"

Ameen means "(Oh Allah) answer our prayer" and/or "so be it." The Prophet ﷺ is reported to have used this phrase after the end of supplications made by others[79] and at the end of *Al-Fatiha* in the prayer.[80]

Now that we have detailed some of the essential manners of crafting a *dua'*, it is important that we examine the most sought-after question about *dua'*: its acceptance. After all, many complain they have never seen the fruits of what they have begged Allah for, even after many attempts and many years of asking. Regarding this, 'Umar رضي الله عنه, the famous companion of the Prophet ﷺ, once said:

> *"I do not carry the worry of acceptance but the worry of dua'.*
> *If I am inspired on how dua' is made, acceptance will*
> *accompany it."*[81]

'Umar رضي الله عنه refers to the magnificent relationship that we have with Allah when we request something of Him: that *dua'* is *guaranteed* to be answered. Yet many of us have asked for things, and either they have not happened yet or they happened in a different way. How could one

---

[79] *Ibn Khuzaymah* #1888; *Jami' at-Tirmidhi*, #3545; *Musnad Ahmad* #7444; Sahih *ibn Hibbaan* #908. *Saheeh al-Jaami'*, 3501. The sources may have slightly different wording. (See: https://islamqa.info/en/26830).

[80] *Sahih al-Bukhari* #6402

[81] Sheikh Saalih al-Fawzaan, *Manners of Dua'*

claim then that *dua'* is *always* answered?

Dua' is answered in one of three ways. Abu Sa'eed Al-Khudri رضي الله عنه reported the Prophet ﷺ said:

> *"There is no Muslim who supplicates to Allah without sin or*
> *cutting family ties in it but that Allah will give him one of*
> *three answers: he will hasten fulfillment of his supplication, he*
> *will store it for him in the Hereafter, or he will divert an evil*
> *from him similar to it." They said, "In that case we will ask*
> *for more." The Prophet said, "Allah has even more."*[82]

Thus, Allah will either grant us what we have asked, save it for us in the Hereafter, or protect us from something evil happening to us. When we raise our hands in *dua'*, we never leave the exchange empty-handed, despite our perception of that at times. When we receive what we have asked, we should be thankful to Allah for granting that to us and be certain that it is good for us. When we are withheld from receiving what we have asked, we should either be patient, as perhaps the answer will be delayed, or we should be *thankful*, as Allah may have withheld from granting us our request because He knows it may not be good for us, even if we cannot perceive it at that time.

Reflect on the *dua'* of Prophet Abraham عليه السلام, when he asked for a prophet to be risen in the lands of Arabia: it was answered *centuries* later in the person of the Prophet Muhammad ﷺ. Hence, patience is required

---

[82] *Musnad Ahmad* #10749. A similar narration is found in *Jami` at-Tirmidhi* #3573.

when we ask, and perhaps withholding what we ask for is actually better for us in this world. Many "unanswered" *dua'* may actually have been acting as a filter, catching all the evil things that may have come our way. Thus, it is possible that without our knowledge we had been under the protection of Allah all along via the *dua'* that we thought went unanswered.

We must strive to realize that Allah has a reason for allowing things to happen when they do. Since we don't have the wisdom, we ask for the best and then trust in Allah's judgment for how our request will be answered. And we trust in Allah to answer however He wishes and ask Him to make us pleased with it.

One may assume it is useless to learn the prior list of etiquette practices of *dua'* if *dua'* is guaranteed to be accepted anyway. Even though sincere *dua'* is guaranteed to be accepted (with the conditions stated above in the hadith), it is still incumbent upon us to learn practices that make it more efficient because, in the end, our goal is to please Allah by emulating the Prophet ﷺ and asking Allah in a way in which He loves. Out of His mercy He gives, but our love—again—should be in that which He loves, rather than in the answer to our requests. Nevertheless, there are certain factors that may prevent *dua'* from being accepted—for example, as mentioned in part of the hadith:

> *"Then he (ﷺ) mentioned [the case] of a man who, having*
> *journeyed far, is disheveled and dusty, and who spreads out his*
> *hands to the sky saying, 'O Lord! O Lord!,' while his food is*
> *haram (unlawful), his drink is haram, his clothing is haram,*

and he has been nourished with haram, so how can [his
supplication] be answered?'[83]

Therefore, we should at least take into account our own actions and make a sincere attempt to rectify our affairs before asking something of Allah. It would be frowned upon to blatantly disrespect a person of whom we ask a favor; we should be ashamed if we treat Allah similarly. In summary, we should try our best to lead a life in accordance with the Laws of Allah while simultaneously asking Him to save us from our mistakes and asking Him to make us successful in our studies.

Let us now proceed to consolidate the technicalities of *dua'* that we have detailed above into an action plan for students:

To make dua' before studying

Put blessing into your work before you start. When making *dua'* before embarking on a study session, we practice an exercise of refocusing our mind on the task at hand, which in turn, helps us focus our attention and clear our minds. Know that your work will be much smoother if you have already asked for Allah's help from the start.

To make dua' while you study

This helps provide an extra "push" when we feel we are dragging our feet during a long study session. During one of your breaks or moments

---

[83] *Sahih Muslim* #1015

of brain fog, take the time and make a one-to-two-minute request of Allah to make it easy. Rest assured that it will be easier after.

To make dua' after you're finished for the day, each day

This wraps up the day and grants you the confidence that Allah will help consolidate into your mind whatever you have studied so that you will retain it and can recall it when needed.

To make dua' for your colleagues

In a time when we often view our colleagues as adversaries and only care about our own success, it is worth another look at what is actually prescribed in our religion. Counterintuitively, we can actually maximize our own chances for a successful score when we make *dua'* for the success of our brothers and sisters. Abu Darda رضي الله عنه reported that the Prophet ﷺ said:

> *"The dua' of a Muslim for his brother in his absence will*
> *certainly be answered. Every time he makes a dua' for good for*
> *his brother, the angel appointed for this particular task says:*
> *'Ameen! May it be for you, too.'"*[84]

For this reason, the more people for whom we make *dua'*, the more *dua'* we receive back for ourselves. Therefore, when asking for the highest grade in the class, ask also for your brothers and sisters to be at the top of the class. By sharing the gift of accomplishment, everyone benefits with multiple *dua'* that are directed at each other and at themselves.

---

[84] This specific wording is quoted from *Riyadh as Saliheen* Book 17 #1495. (Sunnah.com reference: Book 17 #31). Similar narrations are found in *Sahih Muslim* #2732 and #2733.

Imagine that, instead of the constant bickering and infighting among ourselves that has unfortunately become so common, we as Muslims really cared for each other at a personal level and practiced making *dua'* for each other in secret all the time for each other's successes. With this practice alone, imagine how much success would be breathed into our community and how many of our hardships would be alleviated!

To make dua' in your own words in whatever language you like

The *dua'* that always float around on social media during exam times are nice, but sometimes our situation is a little bit different. Make *dua'* personal; everyone's situation is unique. Allah listens to *dua'* no matter who asks and no matter what language is used. Make a personalized *dua'* for yourself, and don't get caught just repeating something you might not understand. Strive to make *dua'* sincerely from the heart. At times, some of us may feel ashamed of our inability to make an intricate *dua'* (e.g., the elaborate, beautiful *dua'* we hear during Ramadan). Instead of feeling ashamed, we should reflect that Allah listens no matter who we are, so we should ask sincerely and stick to making *dua'* to the best of our ability.

In addition, we should make an effort to understand the common *dua'* that are recited, especially the ones that take their basis from the Qur'an and hadith so that we can repeat these *dua'* with sincerity, understand their meaning in the future, and benefit from their comprehensiveness. For example, a student who dreads a public speaking engagement, debate, or oral exam needs only to remember the most famous *dua'* ever made in regards to public speaking. As Allah spoke to Prophet Moses عليه السلام to speak truth to the power of Pharaoh, Prophet Moses عليه السلام asked Allah as follows:

[Moses] said, "My Lord, expand for me my breast [with

assurance]

And ease for me my task

And untie the knot from my tongue

That they may understand my speech."[85]

Thus, any person in any field who is nervous about speaking should emulate Prophet Moses عليه السلام and use it to their advantage so that Allah makes the way clear for them. There are a great many other examples of other prophets and their *dua'*, and it is only to the benefit of ourselves that we seek to learn them and apply them.

To supplicate in times of ease

Many of us increase the intensity of our *dua'* when exams are imminent, and this is natural. If we had the foresight to increase our *dua'* outside exam times and throughout the semester, it would show our sincerity in achieving the goal as the quantity and persistence of our *dua'* would be increased. Show Allah how much achieving success means to you by actively seeking His help when times are easy rather than desperate. Abu Hurairah رضي الله عنه narrated that the Messenger of Allah ﷺ said:

"Whoever wishes that Allah would respond to him during hardship and grief, then let him supplicate plentifully when at ease."[86]

---

[85] Qur'an Chapter 20 ("*Taha*"), verses 25–28
[86] *Jami` at-Tirmidhi* #3382

It is one matter to make *dua'* and remember Allah right before an exam, but it is entirely different when we consistently make *dua'* each time we sit down to study. When we make *dua'* each time we study, specifically to make the material easy for us to understand and to memorize (irrespective of whether this is done during exams or not), and then make a more consolidated, generalized *dua'* for success prior to test day, we maximize our chance for success due to our consistent dedication each day. We should take care to make *dua'* outside exam time so that we show our sincerity to Allah—that we are serious about our request—and not just people who wait until the last minute when it is possibly too late.

Istikhara[87]

It is important for us to frequently practice *istikhara*, and again, the student is in a unique position to practice it often and make it a habit for the rest of their life. *Istikhara* should be made before any major life decision (not just marriage, to which it is often reduced). Indeed, selecting a career path, a school to attend, a city to move to, a job to consider, and a course to take are all major decisions. We need Allah's help to make the right choice, especially if there are two choices that we think would be equally beneficial to us.

Thus, after carefully considering the pros and cons of a decision and taking counsel from family, friends, and experts, we need to trust the decision with Allah by performing *istikhara*. The answer of the *istikhara* will be whatever direction your heart compels you toward—either a confidence

---

[87] Literally meaning: "To seek something that is good from Allah." The Prophet ﷺ taught us to make this specific *dua'* after performing two units of voluntary prayer when seeking to make a decision. See *Sahih al-Bukhari* #1166 for the text of the *dua'*.

to move forward with a decision or a feeling of uncertainty toward it (the answer does not have to come in the form of a dream, as commonly misunderstood). *Istikhara* can be made multiple times until our hearts are confident toward a decision.[88] Employing *istikhara*—making every decision in our life with Allah—in our lives will clarify the benefits of our decisions because we have asked for the best outcome from the Most Merciful. Therefore, our happiness is not tied to landing a dream job or to a project working out; if we had made *istikhara*, we would realize that missing out on these opportunities would actually allow better opportunities to come into our lives.

It is important for us to do well in our education and further cultivate positive growth in our communities; but it is also equally important to stay connected to Allah during challenging times. It is incredibly easy to get lost in the business of the world and in the pages of our textbooks and forget about our duties to Allah as well as His ability to help, listen, and respond.

Dua' has many etiquette practices that could potentially hinder us by making it a complicated worship. Although it shares many similarities with public speaking, we should be careful not to make *dua'* such an elaborate exercise in worship that it loses sincerity and becomes difficult to sustain long-term and consistently. Just as a speech can sound robotic if

---

[88] Sheikh Jangda, Abdul Nasir. "*Istikharah*: How to & Why?" Filmed Dec. 2011. Youtube Video. Posted Dec. 2011. https://www.youtube.com/watch?v=EEcovFTsQ4E

we overprepare, so too can *dua'* become so formulaic that we lose our sincerity while performing it. Although it is recommended that we implement these etiquette practices into our *dua'* so that they are beautifully crafted (and eventually become second nature), the only real prerequisite to making a true and excellent *dua'* is to spill our needs from our heart unto Allah and rely on Him to help us, no matter what language we use or how simple it may be.

Hence, never forget that *dua'* originates from a sincere heart. We should call upon Allah persistently, taking care to keep the line of communication open no matter our current spiritual state. And remember that among the many things we persistently request, seeking forgiveness for shameful deeds is one of the most important requests that *also* propels us toward better study habits.

Say, "O My servants who have transgressed against themselves [by sinning], do not despair of the mercy of Allah. Indeed, Allah forgives all sins. Indeed, it is He who is the Forgiving, the Merciful."

QUR'AN CHAPTER 39 ("THE TROOPS") VERSE 53

6

Toward Seeking Forgiveness

What is the best way to learn—by memorization or understanding? This is an important question, as all subjects require *both* to succeed. Many students complain about their memory and become increasingly frustrated when they are tested on material that can only be memorized but not understood. For example, certain equations or facts about history or human biology can seldom be learned in any other way except rote memorization. In other areas of study, however, much of the material can be learned without memorizing anything—and usually to a better degree when compared to someone who committed themselves to memory alone. What then, is the best way to learn?

To answer which method is superior, we must revisit the recurrent theme of the book: building effective study habits inspired by Islamic practice. In other words, we seek the best of two options and fuse them into a new spiritual category of learning while reviving our lost ambition toward education.

Both learning by memorization and by understanding have their merits and their pitfalls. For example, the one who memorizes without understanding will be inept at applying what is memorized to transcend the text and apply what is learned to the real world. Although they may be able to perfectly recall the details of what they learned, the memorizer will have difficulty adapting to a deviation from the text (even if it has the correct understanding) and will view the deviation as something wrong rather than a contrasting—and correct—viewpoint. In other words, they often limit themselves to a rigid, literal interpretation and find it difficult to accept an alternative, since sometimes it is difficult to extract hidden meanings from a sea of memorized text.

For example, if one memorizes a study that concludes a certain medication has been shown to have a mortality benefit for cardiovascular disease, they would only be able to tell you the details of the articles and regurgitate the concluded results. However, the one who *understands* the study may find that the cited statistics were either overblown (due to an author's implicit bias), forged, or examined in a population different from their current patient population. Their understanding would enable them to interpret the study and decide if the medication would have a mortality benefit in their specific patient population and if the side effects would warrant withholding that medication instead. Thus, the physician who understands may formulate opinions based on their knowledge of medicine and medical journal articles, while the physician who only memorizes will be limited to the facts that pertain to the journal article, sans commentary.

Which would make the better physician?

On the other hand, a person who understands but fails to memorize will have difficulty recalling necessary information to effectively articulate a subject. In addition, certain pertinent facts may be missed that ironically may hinder the understanding of the lesson or cause the person to miss the point entirely. For example, a person who understands *Al-Fatiha* but does not memorize it in Arabic[89] cannot complete even the most basic ritual that every Muslim is required to perform: the prayer. The one who at least memorizes *Al-Fatiha*, even if they do not understand it (though one must make the effort to understand what they read and memorize), can still derive benefit and complete their prayer. Thus, memorization has its merits, especially in mastering concepts at a foundational level (e.g., mathematics, chemistry, anatomy, language, computer science, law, etc.).

To fuse these methods and create a comprehensive way of learning, recognize that learning by understanding and by memorization are two opposite paths that complement each other and lead to the same goal. When unified, they create a harmonious method of learning that is effective, accurate, and applicable. A student who is able to memorize their material *and* understand it is the student best able to not only learn, but to teach others and tackle real-world problems.

But to be perfectly honest, most students prefer understanding over memorization and dread the inevitable exam where they have to memorize detailed facts and answer straight recall "you either know it or you don't" questions. At least with free-answer and essay questions, one can attain

---

[89] English translations are at best an *estimated* explanation of the Arabic text; they will never be able to convey the same effect as the original Arabic.

partial credit by demonstrating their understanding of some of the material, even if their answer is incorrect. Learning by understanding commonly requires a good teacher and a student's sincere, full attention to what is being taught (the student who struggles with understanding should heed the latter point). Identifying the tibia as the fibula, though, won't yield any points for effort or for understanding, even if one knew the answer just half an hour prior. Thus, most students complain about their weak memory and the perceived unfairness of an exam that asks "detailed," seemingly unimportant questions. Faced with this challenge, it is fair to ask: are there spiritual tools that can help improve our memory?

During medical school, I simultaneously began a journey to learn and memorize the Qur'an. After the morning prayer, my breakfast was to read and memorize a set portion of the Qur'an—a few lines—while revising past lessons to ensure I hadn't forgotten them. The rest of the day began only after this habit. Although the initial time crunch created by this habit before school could have led to midday exhaustion from less sleep and the prospect of less effective studying, I found that the direct opposite was occurring. As I flipped through the pages of the Qur'an further and locked them into the recesses of my mind, I found—startlingly—that my ability to remember and retain information from my classes had become more effortless, expansive, and resilient.

This experience illustrates a paradox: that the brain behaves like a muscle. As I exercised it every morning, straining to memorize a few lines, those same lines acted as spiritual dumbbells that strengthened my memory and made memorizing *everything* easier. As Allah has already made the Qur'an easy to remember,[90] it was clear that the additional, un-intended benefit was that it became easier to study and memorize details in other subjects.

After about eighteen months of solid dedication to the Qur'an while simultaneously going to school, I scored near the top of my class in pharmacology. Memorizing the different drugs, pathways, side effects, methods of action, and indications for treatment were seemingly effortless, but I did not accomplish this feat overnight. After all, only a short year earlier I had struggled so mightily with memorizing the bones, muscles, and nerves required for anatomy that I nearly failed the class. My transformation from struggling to memorize human anatomy to becoming one of the top memorizers in pharmacology was in direct correlation with the amount of time I spent with the Qur'an and in direct proportion with the amount of Qur'an I memorized. The truth became evident: if we place Allah first, the rest of our life naturally becomes easier. If only I had learned this truth before, then learning in school via memorization would not have been something dreadful; it would have been part of a simple process that improves all other aspects of life.

Reflect on the people who have committed the Qur'an to memory. If they were to take their memorization and revision seriously from a young age, many of them would establish a foundation to become avid learners and students for the rest of their lives, in any and all disciplines. I would argue that if parents wanted their children to be better students in the secular realm, they would focus less on which private school to send

---

[90] Qur'an Chapter 54 ("*The Moon*"), verse 17

them and instead encourage their children to commit the Qur'an to memory (even just a little, and with the prerequisite that it is not forced). Aided with understanding and application to daily life, we would be on the road to creating more meaningful relationships with our Creator and inevitably more fruitful and purposeful relationships with the rest of creation. This is because the process of memorizing the Qur'an, as with anything that needs to be memorized, requires patience and discipline. These profound character traits are easily inculcated at a young age, but for those of us who are older, it is never too late to learn and apply these traits. And when a person is trained in the Sacred Book and applies it, they will find that they are aided by Allah in ways they could never imagine. What a tremendous gift from Allah to all the memorizers of the Qur'an!

But what if, despite this practice, we still struggle to memorize? Are there other methods to improve our memory? The answer is yes, and indeed one of the fastest ways to improve our memory is by seeking forgiveness.

Just as there are methods to improve our memory, so too are there methods that can negatively affect our memory—methods that are rooted in our actions in day-to-day life away from the classroom. Memory is affected by matters pertaining to our character and worship (for example, our dealings with family and friends and our upholding of duties toward Allah). In other words, our abilities to memorize and to learn are also directly and adversely affected by the sins we commit.

One of the greatest scholars of our community—Imam ash-Shafi'ee—had such an impressive memory that it is reported he memorized the *Muwatta* of Imam Malik (in addition to the Qur'an) by age *ten*.

However, behind this mastery of memory, we see that Imam ash-Shafi'ee held himself to an even higher standard, as he is recorded to have said:

> *I complained to Wakee [his teacher] about my weak memory*
> *and he told me to stop committing sins*
> *and he informed me that knowledge is light*
> *and the light of Allah shall not be given to a sinner.*[91]

Thus, one of the most important Islamic tools for more effective studying is to sincerely attempt to eliminate sinful practices and frequently seek forgiveness. It is imperative that the Muslim student avoid sins as much as possible, and if we fall into a sin or struggle to rid ourselves of a habitual sin, we should continuously and quickly repent after our mistake. After all, we human beings are by nature imperfect, but we should not let that get in the way of attempting betterment. We should be sure that Allah recognizes our efforts to stay away from forbidden actions, with the intentions of pleasing Him and receiving His light. We should never let a sinful action paralyze us; we should let it instead mobilize us to go back to Allah and continue to reach our goals.

If we find ourselves habitually making mistakes and falling into sin, a way to supplement seeking forgiveness is to complement it with a good action. When we sin, sometimes we are quick to lose hope and to guilt ourselves into falling even further. Some people might think, "What's the point of trying to do good? I'm already this bad." This is the wrong attitude.

---

[91] Imam Ibn al-Qayyim, *The Effects of Sins*

The attitude of the Muslim is to immediately refrain from going deeper into sin; instead, we are to take an immediate turn and perform a deed pleasing to Allah, as reported by Abu Dharr رضي الله عنه that the Prophet ﷺ said:

> *"Be mindful of Allah wherever you are, follow a bad deed*
> *with a good deed and it will erase it, and behave with good*
> *character toward people."*[92]

The Prophet ﷺ gives comprehensive advice that transforms a potentially habitual bad deed (or addiction) into a good deed. We will speak in more detail about habit forming in Chapter 10, but as a preview, our sin should be the trigger to do a good deed so that, with time, it becomes a habit. No one is perfect, or else the Prophet ﷺ would not have advised us what to do after committing a sin. Thus, when we follow this paradigm of being mindful of Allah in our actions and complementing bad deeds with good deeds, *inshaAllah,* we will not only replace bad habits with good habits, we will, at the same time, replace bad deeds with good deeds on our scales, contributing to a life of upright moral character.

Similarly, if we feel our religiosity is not up to par, we should never despair because of our shortcomings. The door of Allah is always open; unfortunately, we sometimes shut the door due to our feelings of insecurity and inadequacy. Instead, we should use each mistake as an opportunity to draw closer to Allah through *dua'* by asking for forgiveness. Be

---

[92] *Jami' at-Tirmidhī* #1987

aware, my brothers and sisters, that it is forbidden to despair in the mercy of Allah. No matter how far we are from Islam, it is never too late to come back and start with anything we can offer. It is never too late to ask Allah for help and for guidance, and it is never too late to seek His forgiveness. Allah's mercy far outweighs any and all sins we have committed, even if they fill the earth to the sky and are multiplied by the number of people in human history. Reflect on the following verse:

> *"Say, 'O My servants who have transgressed against*
> *themselves [by sinning], do not despair of the mercy of*
> *Allah. Indeed, Allah forgives all sins. Indeed, it is He who is*
> *the Forgiving, the Merciful.'"*[93]

Allah will never close this door, even for the student who is far away from Him, ignoring His commandments and living his own way. It is imperative for the one who engages in actions that are detrimental to themselves in this world and the Hereafter—including but not limited to partying; using tobacco, drugs, and/or alcohol; and participating in illicit relationships—that they try their best to stay away from these and make amends by forming new habits . These activities lead to physical and emotional problems that affect our willpower to study (among other harmful effects they have on our lives in the present with consequences in the future). They also occupy a significant amount of precious free time that could be used for studying. If a person makes the effort to leave this lifestyle

---

[93] Qur'an Chapter 39 (*"The Troops"*), verse 53

behind them—a life of temporary pleasure with serious negative repercussions—they will find their free time increased and their productivity boosted. An additional incentive is that when a person leaves these sins for the sake of Allah and strives to seek forgiveness, their sins will be replaced with good deeds, as Allah mentions:

> *"Except for those who repent, believe, and do righteous work. For them Allah will replace their evil deeds with good. And ever is Allah Forgiving and Merciful."*[94]

If we feel that it is too difficult to leave these habits (perhaps they have become addictions), then we may need to reflect on the seriousness of the potential grave consequences of our actions and consider seeking professional help. We should not, however, ever despair in the hope that Allah can change our condition if we are sincere. One only needs to reflect that Allah changed the heart of a person who was on his way to *kill* the Prophet ﷺ to one of the greatest leaders in Muslim history, 'Umar ibn al-Khattab رضي الله عنه. Be cognizant then, of the fact that unchecked sins are often the source of difficulties in life, such as being subjected to oppressive rulers and overall communal defeat.

Additionally, do not fall for shaytan's tricks, such as telling you to be religious when you are older or when you are free from studies. The time to return to Allah is now. The Muslim student specifically is in a wonderful position to return to Him because they have youth, energy, and free

---

[94] Qur'an Chapter 25 ("*The Criterion*"), verse 70

time on their side to practice worship and the ideals of Islam while examining the deeds at which they excel and those upon which they need to improve. Another benefit to seeking forgiveness is that it will result in an increase in our *rizq* (provision, livelihood).[95] Therefore, the student who perpetually seeks forgiveness will be well on their way to establishing a profitable investment in this world (through their grades, career, wealth, and family) and in the Hereafter.

Therefore, youth, take advantage of the time afforded to you to learn your religion and come back to Allah, no matter how far away you are or what you have done in your past or continue to do in the present. It will benefit not only you, but the entire community through your latent talents. And it will not only benefit you in this world, but it will also benefit you on the Day of Judgment as one of the people under the shade of Allah.[96]

There are many ways to seek forgiveness; chief, of course, is to simply ask Allah in the form of *dua'* and make the necessary changes in our lifestyle to avoid repeating the same mistake. However, many other easy (and seemingly insignificant) actions can also lead to forgiveness. For example, sins are forgiven upon greeting another Muslim and shaking their hand, as reported by the companion Al-Bara' ibn 'Azib رضي الله عنه that the Prophet ﷺ said:

> *"Two Muslims will not meet and shake hands having their*

---

[95] Qur'an Chapter 71 ("*Noah*"), verses 10-12
[96] *Sahih Muslim* #1031

sins forgiven them before they separate."[97]

Similarly, perfecting *wudu'*,[98] engaging in prayer, and actively re-membering Allah are all wonderful opportunities to seek forgiveness. As for *wudu'*, it is reported that the Prophet ﷺ stated that the sins of each body part being washed will be forgiven (with the exception of major sins, which require repentance).[99] If a person becomes a person of prayer, then they have another added benefit as their sins are forgiven between every prayer, the two Friday prayers, and between two Ramadans.[100] Addition-ally, performing specific *dhikr*[101] after each prayer will result in the for-giveness of sins, even if they are too numerous to be counted, like the foam of the sea.[102] Also, the one who observes Ramadan unlocks three different ways of attaining full expiation of all their sins (specifically, if they fast during the month, stand in prayer nightly for the month, or pray in the night of power during the month).[103] Thus, we should not let the per-ceived difficulty of studying during Ramadan hinder us from fasting dur-ing it, from standing in prayer nightly for it, or from seeking the night of power in the last ten odd nights; these activities will only make us better students with additional blessings.

Lastly, it is worth noting that if we would hope for Allah's forgiveness,

---

[97] *Sunan Abi Dawud* #5212

[98] Islamic ritual washing (ablution) of certain parts of the body

[99] *Sahih Muslim* #244

[100] *Sahih Muslim* #233

[101] Remembrance for the sake of Allah

[102] *Sahih Muslim* #597. Also see *Sahih al-Bukhari* #6405 for an example of another easy *dhikr* with similar reward

[103] *Sahih al-Bukhari* #1901 and *Sahih al-Bukhari* #2008

we should be mindful to forgive others, especially those who have wronged us. It is possible that we continue to perform underwhelmingly in school because we have not yet let go of some long-forgotten grudge or because we hold someone in contempt. Seek instead to forgive and move on; life is too short to dwell on the mistakes of others, as Allah states:

"And let not those of virtue among you and wealth swear not to give [aid] to their relatives and the needy and the emigrants for the cause of Allah, and let them pardon and overlook. Would you not like that Allah should forgive you? And Allah is Forgiving and Merciful."[104]

Therefore, strive to live a life that is in accordance with what Allah loves so that through His love you may find success in the present life and in the next—not only for yourself, but for the entire Muslim community.

The debate between understanding or memorizing study material should be a nonissue for the student utilizing Islamic tools because, for them, it is a matter of using *both* to excel in study. As they seek to understand, they listen with a sincere heart and attentive ear, seeking to apply the lessons to their life or later in their studies or career, rather than forget it at semester's end. As they seek to improve their memory, they live a life guarding against sin, exercising their brain by memorizing the words of Allah, and continuously seeking forgiveness; perhaps these actions will cause blessings to enter their life and enable them to memorize anything they wish with ease.

---

[104] Qur'an Chapter 24 ("*The Light*"), verse 22

If the student struggles with their memory, they should examine their character and mannerisms, as well as their treatment of their parents, the general public, and their relationship with Allah. They ought to take themselves to account: *Am I performing my prayers on time? Have I checked in with my parents recently? What sins did I commit today? What can I do to be better tomorrow? Is there anyone in need that I can help?* With this type of sincere self-reflection, they are able to rectify their affairs and return to Allah, seeking His nearness, and in the pursuit of returning to Allah, they will be rewarded with what they need in this world (for example, the ability to memorize better and the attainment of better scores and a decent career) while they are simultaneously brought closer to their religion and to Allah—by being forgiven, being given good deeds in replacement of their sins, and being guided to better deeds—with the hope of an even *better* reward in the Hereafter.

Glory be to Allah! How merciful is Allah! How subtle is Allah in His affairs! Because He still loved us and wanted us to be close to Him even though we were far from Him, He caused us to struggle with learning and memorizing because He knew this struggle was important to us, and that we would find any means necessary to overcome it. And even after going to everyone else for help first, we finally found the answers with Allah, and in so doing sought His help and forgiveness. As a result of returning to Allah, He grants us what we need in this world, and He has prepared Paradise in the Hereafter!

Is there anything else that the slave of Allah can say after this, except *alhamdulillah*?

"And (remember) when your Lord proclaimed, 'If you are grateful, I will surely increase you (in favor); but if you deny, indeed, My punishment is severe.'"

QUR'AN CHAPTER 14 ("ABRAHAM"), VERSE 7

7

An Attitude of Gratefulness

The issue of gratitude came to the forefront amidst another high-stakes final during the end of my second year of medical school during yet another finals week. My performance would now determine if I was ready for the United States medical licensing exam (US-MLE) —a huge factor in placement for training programs—and if I was ready to become a full-fledged physician. Each question felt harder than that for which I had prepared, the exams tested concepts I thought were insignificant details, and I lamented that the supplemental practice material was not as similar to the exam as promised. As I exited the exam and the knots started to twirl in my stomach and anxiety poured in, questions such as "Will I pass?" dominated my thoughts for the rest of the day. In the past, I always tried to thank Allah after exams, but usually only *after* receiving the result. This highlighted the fact that I wasn't *truly* grateful—my gratefulness was contingent upon a good result.

This time felt different. Even though I had not received my results, in the moment I returned home, Allah guided me to thank Him immediately as I performed the prostration of gratefulness.[105] Perhaps I did so out of fear, hoping this deed would get me the desired result, or perhaps it was a realization of my insincerity. It was, after all, He who brought me to this point and enabled me to finish my exam, giving me the chance to become a physician. As much as I feared the result, I resolved that I would remain thankful and content whatever the result would be, while containing my anxiety by trusting my affairs in the hands of Allah. In hindsight, my previous actions of watchful waiting before being thankful actually reflected an attitude of ungratefulness. I realized that prostrating at this time, when my need was great and I had no idea how I would actually do on my test, produced a more genuine attitude of gratefulness, initiated with optimism; fueled by hope.

Six months later, I found myself opening my results for USMLE Step 1, and with a sigh of relief, I saw that I had not only passed, but that I had scored in the 99th percentile. Again, I found myself with my head on the floor as I performed the prostration of gratefulness.

Through this experience, I realized that as the slave of Allah continues to thank Him for His blessings, they find that they are, in fact, being given more blessings. Too often, many of us get lost in our own ego by relying on our own limited ability, and based on that perceived ability, we are proud of the result. No matter how much we have studied, dedicated to class time, or memorized, the undeniable truth is that we are products of

---

[105] See footnote 110 near the end of this chapter

whatever Allah grants us. Further, every human would love to succeed, but more than success, we love *continued* success. One of the shortest, easiest paths to success—and indeed to Allah—is through the regular practice of gratitude, as He explains:

> *"And [remember] when your Lord proclaimed, 'If you are grateful, I will surely increase you [in favor]; but if you deny, indeed, My punishment is severe.'"[106]*

Allah presents a simple formula. He tells us that if we are grateful, we will see an increase; the beauty of the formula, however, is that He did not specify *what* would be increased. This means that if we foster an attitude of gratefulness (for example, being grateful for our health), perhaps we will be increased in our health or, alternatively, in our wealth. Hence, if we want to be increased in our success in school, we should thank Allah for the grades we have *right now*. If we would like a higher salary, then we should thank Allah for the amount that we are receiving *right now*. If we want contentment in our lives, then we should reflect on the many blessings we are afforded and thank Allah for each of them *in the present*. Whatever we may desire, Allah has given us the formula to not only obtain it but to increase its amount (or increase in goodness in other parts of our life). To put it simply, an attitude of gratefulness is fostered by training our minds to weed out the negative and to focus on the positive, tangible things that we have in our life and be thankful for them.

---

[106] Qur'an Chapter 14 ("*Abraham*"), verse 7

Focusing on the positive and weeding out the negative are necessary prerequisites on the path of learning gratitude. For example, a student may claim this book is useless and that they still struggle with school, despite applying the Islamic study tools outlined in this book. With this negative mindset, they will develop a negative emotional state that fails to focus on breeding success; they will be too busy placing the blame on what they feel was a useless book. Instead, we must strive to focus on the positive. Perhaps the advice in this book did not lead you to success in school, but hopefully it taught you important concepts toward leading a better Islamic life. Or perhaps it helped a friend who was struggling or led you to find a better book about improving your scores in school. Isn't that, at least, something to be happy about? Can we thank Allah that He provided a means for someone else to succeed or that we learned something about Allah we previously did not know?

We often have plenty of things to complain about—a bad teacher, a missed alarm, subpar coffee, or a boring lecture—but flooding our minds with negative thoughts negatively impacts our ability to study. Instead, we should try to look for the positives. Does the teacher make good Power-Points? Maybe the lecture has useful points that are pertinent to the exam, even if it is boring. Overlook that the coffee was subpar and focus on the fact that Allah gave you enough money to pay for it.

Training our mind to ignore negative impulses and replacing them with positive messages and healthier outlooks is a *necessary* shift in mindset. When we have less to complain about, we enable a more positive, healthy lifestyle that will motivate us to study more efficiently. Specifically, when we cease blaming external factors for our problems, we can start to internalize our own weaknesses and address them honestly, enabling us to embark on rectifying those weaknesses and to stay committed to our craft, no matter the odds and no matter the situation in which we are placed.

This formula for success is counterintuitive to what is popular in our current culture regarding seeking success. To get what we want, we often focus on the object we are *seeking* rather than on what we already have. For example, we focus on the fact that we don't have an A grade in our class; as a result, we do everything in our power to get that A. While there is nothing inherently wrong with this attitude, we cannot just focus on the means to the goal. Rather, Allah teaches us to focus on what we already have, and through being grateful for what we have, we will be increased and may inevitably achieve what we don't have—by Allah's will. In other words, Allah knows that we want more, but if we *truly* want more, we should be thankful so that He can increase us and give us more.

For example, imagine a father gifts a laptop to his son as a graduation gift. Imagine the son takes the laptop, says thank you, and then places it in the attic. A few years later he comes back and asks his father for an upgraded model of the same laptop. Unless we are angels, most of us would find it impossible to gift this person another laptop because he didn't use the first one at all. The father would be more likely to give his son an upgraded model if he actually used the laptop, and even then, only if he really benefited from it. If after he had gifted the original laptop his son used it to further his career and learn new skills, perhaps he would not even wait for his son to ask for a newer model and gift it out of the joy that he was using the original gift in positive ways! And to Allah is the greatest example.

Therefore, to work within the blessings that Allah has given us—by being mindful of Allah and using the blessings He has given us in the proper way—is the truest form of expressing gratitude. For example, a film producer might express gratitude by making documentaries for the sake of Allah that raise awareness about social ills and their solutions. Perhaps your intelligence in the field of science prompts you to research new renewable energy sources that are more cost-effective and safer for the environment. Perhaps your beautiful voice could be used for the recitation of the Qur'an, and perhaps someone's faith would be increased because of that. Thus, we show thanks not just through the tongue and the heart; it is imperative that we also express it through *action*. Allah highlights this point:

> *"They made for him what he willed of elevated chambers, statues, bowls like reservoirs, and stationary kettles. [We said], 'Work, O family of David, in gratitude.' And few of My servants are grateful."*[107]

As explained by Imam al-Ghazali, somewhere along this spectrum—with the highest point being using our gifts for the sake of Allah—we are divided into three levels of gratefulness. The first is to simply be happy about the blessing itself (for example, food on the table). A person with this attitude would be happy if they had food on their table, no matter

---

[107] Qur'an Chapter 34 ("*Sheba*"), verse 13

who prepared it; their happiness is tied to the *food* itself. This is a poor form of thanks as it fails to recognize the One who provided it.

The second level is to recognize that Allah gave us a blessing, and because of the fact that Allah gave us that blessing, we are joyful because of the greatness of the One who granted it to us. At this level, happiness and thankfulness are tied to the *Giver*, rather than the actual *gift* itself. It is similar to receiving an awful family portrait from your young daughter. There have been better portraits with more accurate representations, but despite this, we are so overjoyed with the *thought* and the one who drew it and gave it to us that we hang it up on our fridge for everyone to see.

The third and most perfect level of gratitude is when a person more deeply contemplates his blessings and asks, "*Why* did Allah grant *me* this?" We examine the blessing and realize that He granted this blessing so that we can *use* it as a means to get nearer to Him. Thus, our computer becomes a blessing that is used in the service of learning about Islam and to benefit our work, rather than simply as a form of entertainment. The family portrait becomes a means to make *dua'* for Allah to bless our legacy. When we eat, we pay attention not just to the blessing of having food on our table but also to *how* we eat it, imitating the Prophet ﷺ in his tableside manner in hopes of enveloping our lives in the curtains of worship with actions that Allah loves.[108]

Take, for example, Allah granting a person the opportunity to practice medicine. After their long years of school, a medical student can start

---

[108] Imam al-Ghazali, *The Revival of the Religious Sciences*. The above explanations and examples are supplemented by the following source with different examples: Ustadh Elwan, Hassan. "Understanding Gratitude." Aug. 2016. Youtube Video, 28:00. Posted Aug. 2016. https://www.youtube.com/watch?v=3Q77s6_adcc

to practice medicine simply for the sake of prestige or the potential financial benefits of being a physician; their joy is simply in those worldly prizes. Whether their practice is ethical, correct, or evidence-based is secondary.

However, a wiser medical student realizes that the gift of being able to care for patients is from Allah, and they recognize that Allah is the One who gave them the opportunity to practice medicine. As a result, they appreciate their gift of practicing medicine, internalizing their thanks and doing their best to practice medicine with the highest ethical, intellectual, and moral standard, even when burned out. They realize that not everyone is allowed this privilege, so they focus on the positive aspects of their career while overlooking the negative.

The wisest medical student, however, will ask, "How can I get closer to Allah by practicing medicine?" They will then find their own specific calling and work toward that end, continuously seeking Allah through their work, showing their thankfulness through action. That is what mobilizes them to treat patients with respect and dignity, to learn treatments and be aware of specific side effects, and to go beyond the call of duty in caring for their patients. They may feel bad that their fasting, prayer, or other good deeds are not as good as others who commit to them, so they use the gift of practicing medicine as worship and realize that perhaps Allah granted them this gift to make up for the ritualistic deeds in which they are deficient. They work with excellence because it doesn't matter if they get recognition for their work or some other material benefit; they find value in themselves and in their work. They try their best to seek innovative ways to use their blessing in the pursuit of the pleasure of Allah.

This is the Muslim who contemplates the necessary actions for each gift that Allah grants them in order to get closer to Him. We ask Allah to enable us to live and work in our careers to these lofty standards.

When the Muslim student understands that thankfulness to Allah is manifested in actions within the blessings they already have and that increasing their thankfulness will invite more success, they are subsequently increased in success in every aspect of their life. They enter a select group amongst the *few*, the servants of Allah who are truly thankful.

But what if we do not receive the things we ask for and find dead ends on projects we feel were meant for us, even while practicing an attitude of gratefulness?

To fully understand the answer, we must remind ourselves of our inherent relationship with Allah. Specifically, that Allah is our Master and may grant us many gifts, but we as humans—slaves to our Master—are not entitled to any of these gifts. Whatever we receive from our Master is a gift, not compensation. When our Master chooses to withhold something from us, either it was better for us not to have it or it was simply not meant for us. In other words, we are not entitled to it, even if we think it would be the best thing for us.

If you reflect on your own life, you may find situations in which you wished for something to have happened one way, but it happened the opposite way. Eventually, after many years, you realized that the opposite way actually turned out better, while your preferred way may have been detrimental to you. Thus, sometimes there are blessings in failure and in struggles, whether we realize it or not.

To illustrate this concept, I will share a personal reflection from my own life. I graduated high school with a GPA of 4.4. Coupled with good SAT scores and extracurricular activities, I was accepted into every university to which I applied. After researching all the options and assessing how each university would help my end goal of becoming a physician, I chose the University of California Riverside (to the shock of my high school colleagues, teachers, and counselors as they thought I would select a more prestigious university). At the time, UCR had a program with UCLA for their medical school that was open only to UCR undergraduates that I thought would be a fantastic way of circumventing the disproportionate odds of getting into medical school the traditional way, and increasing my chances to attend a prestigious medical school. As I mentioned earlier, certain factors closed the road for me to get into this program, and I eventually went overseas to complete my medical degree.

Only after many years pass and our sadness over perceived missed opportunities wanes do we come to understand greater wisdom. Had I chosen a more prestigious school than UCR, I would not have met honest, sincere mentors and friends that shaped my life toward a different path. Specifically, my undergraduate experience enabled me to make one of the most important decisions in my life: to fall in love with Islam and commit to it to the best of my ability. Every decision I have made since this stems from this decision. Hence, it was not a "failure" to have gone to UCR (even though I was not admitted into the UCR-UCLA program); rather, it was a necessary route in my spiritual development.

Perhaps if I had gone to another university, I would have strayed farther from the path of Islam simply because I would have focused more on my studies. Further, had I not failed with respect to the UCR-UCLA program,

I would have never experienced going overseas for medical school. I would not have had the opportunity to experience life in different cities of the world or the opportunity to meet even more wonderful role models. I *had* to fail for Allah to increase me in other parts of my life. And perhaps because I had a chip on my shoulder by graduating from an overseas program, I studied twice as hard for my board exam as I would have (had I been in a U.S. school) which is what ultimately led to success on my exam, completing my residency program, and eventually working as a full-time physician.

My experience illustrates the point that sometimes what we plan on being perfect scenarios in our lives are, in fact, not perfect scenarios. Somewhere along the line we realize some wisdom for not being able to go down a preferred route, as Allah explains:

> *"… But perhaps you hate a thing and it is good for you;*
> *and perhaps you love a thing and it is bad for you. And*
> *Allah Knows, while you know not."*[109]

When we look at our lives and reflect on the path on which Allah takes us, few words can describe the feeling: one is *subhanAllah* as we marvel at the twists and turns it takes; the second is *alhamdulillah* for the end results. Be mindful then, reader, and realize that every experience— every failure, blocked path, opened door, missed opportunity, new acquaintance—is no accident. Rather, these are the means by which we

---

[109] Qur'an Chapter 2 ("*The Cow*"), part of verse 216

understand ourselves in a confusing world, a means of reflection and opportunities to thank Allah. With this knowledge, the Muslim is at peace, and everything that happens to them is good for them.

Furthermore, whenever something good happens to us and we feel excited or happy, or whenever something terrible is averted, it is a good habit to remind ourselves that everything happens with Allah's decree. One of the best ways to practically thank Allah right away is to practice saying *alhamdulillah* as part of our common vocabulary, and an easy action to learn is the prostration of thankfulness. This is directly from the example of the Prophet ﷺ.[110] It is performed similar to the prostration done when reciting some verses of the Qur'an, and the student is encouraged to look further into the details of performing it.

To summarize, one of the easiest paths to Allah is thankfulness. As we traverse the path to Allah by being grateful, we realize that we are increased in success in our day-to-day lives—in all parts of our lives. We develop an attitude of gratefulness by first asking Allah to enable us to be grateful, training our minds to focus on the positive, moving past the negative, and performing appropriate actions with the blessings we have been given. We use our eyes to read, our ears to listen, and our computers to study, and we protect ourselves from sinning through these gifts we have been given.

Anyone on this path knows that this is a lifelong journey, so it would be wise for the student to consider their time in school as their practice ground. Instead of lamenting your terrible performance this semester, be

---

[110] *Sunan ibn Majah* #1394 (see also *Jami` at-Tirmidhi* #1578)

thankful that you have an opportunity to bounce back. Then get up and do the work, be thankful for the journey, and in the end, you may find increase in your performance in school and in your position with Allah—a beautiful balance that benefits you in this world and the Hereafter.

"And thus we have made you a middle community that you will be witnesses over the people and the Messenger will be a witness over you. And We did not make the qiblah which you used to face except that We might make evident who would follow the Messenger from who would turn back on his heels. And indeed, it is difficult except for those whom Allah has guided. And never would Allah have caused you to lose your faith. Indeed Allah is, to the people, Kind and Merciful."

QUR'AN CHAPTER 2 ("THE COW") VERSE 143

8

Balance

In life, there is a constant battle between choosing to perform actions we *need* to do and choosing actions we *want* to do. Seldom do we find people who have aligned what they need to do with what they want to do, but when it is done, it creates harmony and happiness in life that would be otherwise very difficult to attain. For many of us, studying for school is often what we need to do, but not necessarily what we would like to be doing at certain times. As we are immersed in a more diverse, technologically driven era where the number of distractions seems endless, it is critically important for any student to find balance—but especially so for the Muslim student.

One of the most powerful driving forces that helps create a culture of procrastination around studying is the inherent fear of the amount of time, effort, and work it takes to study. Because of the negative image studying connotes in many of our minds—for example, of people locking themselves in their rooms for entire days, coming out only for the necessities of food and water, sacrificing their time with their family and friends, and overall living a boring, unfulfilling life—we feed our mind a toxic interpretation of studying that naturally results in our inability to motivate ourselves to open our books.

Growing up, I was convinced that I would drive myself insane if I ever had to go through days of studying as described above. Eventually, as I ventured into medical school and found many of my colleagues exhibiting similar behavior patterns, I believed there had to be a better way—a better way to find balance in a time when many students pack their belongings in the early morning and head to the libraries and study spaces to spend the ensuing day (and possibly night) buried in their textbooks, leaving the beautiful breeze and the comfort of their pillows far behind.

Is this amount of sacrifice needed to study successfully? Do these habits actually translate to better grades? And if they don't, then can studying be done more effectively and with less stress?

The truth is, these study habits may translate to better grades, but I argue they will also negatively impact our mental health and happiness. Human beings are social creatures. We need personal time and social time to interact with our family, friends, and circles of influence. We need time to relax, sleep, and enjoy hobbies concurrently with the time we spend working. But we also need to be aware that distractions like social media, video games, and television can negatively impact not only our work but our *desire* to work.

In this chapter, we seek to summarize the advice of our Prophet ﷺ

about finding balance within worship and apply this to our lives as students struggling to balance our studies with the responsibilities of life, ultimately, learning to change our perception of studying entirely. It is narrated by 'Abdullah ibn 'Amr ibn Al-'As رضي الله عنهم that the Prophet ﷺ said:

> *"'O 'Abdullah! Have I not been informed that you fast all the*
> *day and stand in prayer all night?' I said, 'Yes, O Allah's*
> *Messenger (ﷺ)!' He said, 'Do not do that! Observe the fast*
> *sometimes and also leave them (the fast) at other times; stand*
> *up for the prayer at night and also sleep at night. Your body*
> *has a right over you, your eyes have a right over you and your*
> *wife has a right over you.'"*[111]

The Prophet ﷺ explains here (and in another, similar narration[112]) that when we overburden ourselves with worship, we may be prone to fatigue and unable to persevere in our worship. Such imbalance in religious devotion eventually leads to the deterioration of our personal health and responsibilities, notably by neglecting the rights of others.

To succeed in anything in life, we must commit to diligent practice, hard work, honest effort, and unwavering discipline. In this pursuit, many of us either work our bodies to the point that our ability to persevere is compromised, or we completely neglect our bodies and fall victim to the dangers of a sedentary lifestyle. Living an Islamic lifestyle demands that its

---

[111] *Sahih al-Bukhari* #5199
[112] *Sunan Abi Dawud* #1369

adherents find balance (to the best of their ability). For the student, this requires balancing worship and studying for school. What we find, however, are many personality types in the sea of Muslim students across campuses around the globe. The following are some of the personalities I have personally noticed—and have myself been a part of—over my career in academics and to which I have alluded in previous chapters.

The first is the overzealous Muslim who expends so much time and effort in their worship, in the affairs of their organization (e.g., as an MSA board member), and for their community (e.g., being involved in a number of volunteer activities) that they do not have the time nor the energy to study. In other words, their many commitments keep them from succeeding in school. These struggles then frustrate them (and perhaps their family) and create a strain that affects their health, worship, and commitments. In fact, because they are scrambling for time to make up for their struggles in school and staying in touch with their commitments, they probably will overlook their exercise routine and eating habits, further exacerbating the harm to their overall well-being. Thus, what they consume becomes harmful, their worship is tainted with the distractions of not succeeding in school, and they are unhappy as they have to spend time with the books rather than with the people they desire to serve.

The second personality is the nonpracticing Muslim who neglects their worship altogether and focuses only on studying, relying on their merits and ability alone. This student has two potential paths (within a spectrum). On the first (and dangerous path), Allah will allow them to succeed, which means that person will become even more deluded by their perceived ability to succeed rather than realizing Who endowed them with that ability. On the second potential path, they will fail on their own merit and ability, and if Allah has mercy on them, He may cause the student to fail so that they could turn back in His remembrance, resulting in a deeper spiritual relationship with Allah, which results in success in the spiritual and physical realms.

The third personality is the overly anxious student, the one who is so worried about their grades and who is constantly consumed by doubts and fears of being left behind in their studies that they—out of sincere concern for their studies—misplace their time with their worship and neglect their health in the pursuit of studying. This type of student is never satisfied and always in a constant state of worry; in other words, they live between exams. They are constantly canceling get-togethers, missing family events, and always "behind" in their studies. This behavior affects their quality of life by placing undue strain on their most important relationships— namely, their family and friends. They also feel guilty about missing their worship, but they may create excuses (such as not being "smart" enough to get good grades and live a balanced life with religion at the same time) to warrant their behavior.

The fourth personality is the gambler, the Muslim student who prepares nothing in the way of studying and relies on Allah just before their finals. Their actions are as useless as trying to put out a fire without water. This student also has two potential pathways on a spectrum: either they will realize the error of their ways and start to commit to the necessary work before relying on Allah, thus reaping success because of it, or they will blame Allah for their misfortune and be led further astray.

However, there is an elusive fifth personality who is able to find balance in their worship and in life, and these are the most successful among us. This is the Muslim student who, realizing they have a responsibility to their Creator, engages in the obligatory acts of worship and as much voluntary worship as they can. By doing so, they give up the reins of their ego and place their trust in Allah first and in their own ability second to master the material. They realize that Allah is the ultimate source of success. If they start with Allah first, then they have started in the most correct way. They realize that they must take care of the rights of their body, their eyes, their family, their guests, and the rest of the people. By doing so, they create a harmony between their worship and their personal life that enables them to arrive to their study time fresh and ready to learn.

There are two potential pathways within a spectrum for this student also, but in contrast with the gambler and the non-practicing Muslim, both pathways breed success. Firstly, this student may find that they have continued success as a student and are able to balance the rights of their Creator and the creation, for which they are thankful. Because of their thankfulness, Allah increases them even more. Conversely, they may struggle despite taking care of their rights, but they persevere and are patient with Allah's decree. As a result, Allah is with them and that is better for them. This student accepts their limited ability to see the big picture and understands that Allah might withhold something that appears to be good out of His mercy, just as a parent sometimes withholds junk food from their children. Thus, they are not overly dismayed by a bad test result, and they are not extremely overjoyed about a good test result. They understand the ebb and flow of life and remain in a state between thanks and patience as much as possible.

This personality may seem out of reach, but that would be doubting our inherent potential, and we know that Allah does not burden us with that which we cannot bear. This personality is the goal—not the norm—and there are several levels within it. For our purposes, it would be helpful to identify our own personality and shortcomings as students while learning from this personality and how the balance of rights directly affects our study habits.

This brings us to the main question and discussion about the hadith of the Prophet ﷺ mentioned earlier. How does taking care of the rights of the body, the eyes, the family, neighbors, guests, employers, and the rest of creation help make us better students? Specifically, we seek to learn the lesson of not overburdening ourselves with worship (directly from the hadith), and then apply this concept to our lives as students. To this end, we will mention each of these rights and how it pertains to finding balance in our life as students.

As for the rights of the body, for our practical purposes as students, we must not neglect what we consume, and we must remind ourselves of the importance of its upkeep with exercise. As for the eyes, they require sleep to help consolidate our learning and provide us rest. As for our family, positive relationships with our parents, spouse, and siblings will provide us with the support we need to persevere in difficult times while simultaneously increasing our *rizq*. And as for our guests and the rest of creation, this is another opportunity to provide social balance in times where we may feel socially isolated during our studies.

The Rights of the Body

Many of my colleagues would be dismayed during exams because their commitment to studying inevitably led to a sedentary lifestyle that contributed to getting out of shape and gaining weight. I wanted to change this routine and try something different. Instead of being cooped up in the library for the entire day, even during the days before exams, I focused on maintaining the same daily routine I was already practicing. That meant that if every Thursday was basketball night, I played basketball, even if it was for an extended period of time. If I was eating healthy during the beginning of the semester, I wasn't ordering daily pizza during finals week. Some of my colleagues were shocked at the perceived risk of "wasting" time on the court rather than with my nose in the books. But when the time came for exams, I continued to move forward with everyone else, despite the time I had "wasted" on my hobbies.

It may be a surprising revelation that a person can enjoy their hobbies during finals week and still keep up with the rest of the student body. Truthfully, it's not because a person is inherently intelligent that they are able to live this balanced lifestyle. When a person keeps up with their exercise, hobbies, and diet, they naturally create a positive atmosphere in their life. As a result, they *feel* happier. Giving the body its due right by taking care not to expend too much time studying and wearing it out enables us to arrive at our place of study with a refreshed mind (rather than an annoyed one) that will help us achieve great focus. This is because our distractions are out of the way (for me, playing basketball) and not unconsciously (and constantly) trying to pry us away from the books. So instead of spending fifteen hours in the library *intermittently* studying, complaining about tests, gossiping with our "study groups," and checking social media, a better alternative is to spend three to five (or whatever number needed) *quality* hours studying and to use the rest of the time however we like.

Thus, whatever activities we enjoy doing during the weeks before finals—whether it's sports, weight lifting, running, yoga, reading, writing, or even video games—we need to be sure to keep up with our hobbies even during finals (within reasonable limits). This will help balance our life to ensure we have a focused mind and refreshed body, ready to study efficiently when it is demanded of us.

I should caution those whose interests are solely sedentary to have some type of outdoor activity. Even if it is just a leisurely stroll around the block, keeping the body active releases our natural endorphins that enable a state of positivity that motivates us to study. The added benefit is that we contribute to the upkeep of our body (and health) via exercise.

Another possible contributing factor to gaining weight during exam time is the challenge many people face during exams: controlling what we eat. Whether it's the daily granola bar, comfort foods like chocolate or candy, or tons of sugary juices or coffee to stay awake, everything we eat directly affects our ability to learn, store energy, and be successful.

Be careful not to train your body to eat while you are actively studying. Just as Pavlov's dog was conditioned to salivate in the presence of the lab technician who normally fed him rather than in response to the food itself, we may unknowingly condition our bodies to become hungry during an exam. This may result in unwanted distractions during our actual exam, and the last thing anyone wants is to think about M&Ms while trying to answer a hard question. Usually no food is allowed during the exam, so what ends up happening is that instead of focusing on the answers to the questions, we are so distracted by the fact that we didn't have enough time to eat breakfast or that we don't have our favorite binge snacks that we cannot properly focus on the exam. Choosing to forgo snacking while actively studying and deferring it to break time will prevent this possible conditioning, allowing for fewer distractions during studying and more focused test taking.

But more important than choosing *when* to eat is focusing on *what* to eat, especially when considering sugar rushes with quick burnout or the dreaded food coma. Nutritious foods that are advisable to eat during study breaks include high-protein foods, such as nuts, cheese, and eggs. If you have a sweet tooth, opt for the natural sugar in fruits, such as apples and bananas, rather than a Snickers from the vending machine.

Another important consideration is the amount of water we consume. Staying hydrated is quite possibly the fastest, safest, and easiest way to cure fatigue. This is because many of us unknowingly become dehydrated when we study long hours and either forget to drink water or drink *only* natural diuretics like coffee. In other words, dehydration contributes to fatigue. A good way to tell if you are dehydrated is to ask yourself if you're thirsty. As a rule, if one is already thirsty, it is an indication of dehydration.

So how much water should we be drinking? The National Academies of Sciences, Engineering, and Medicine determined that an adequate intake of fluids (from water, other beverages and food) for men is roughly about fifteen cups (three liters) of total beverages a day and about eleven cups for women.[113] When we substitute water for other types of beverages we commonly consume during exam times, we will tap into our natural, untapped energy reserve that will lead to incredible results, including (but not limited to) prevention of muscle fatigue, improved skin texture, maintaining normal excretory function, controlling calories (by limiting sugary drinks), and saving money. An additional (and environmentally conscious) tip that will help us track our water consumption is to invest in a reusable water bottle, which helps reduce waste incurred from one-time-use plastic bottles and at the same time easily track how much we consume in a day. If you are a student combatting fatigue, there is perhaps no greater beverage than water.

The discussion about what we consume would not be complete without mentioning the phenomenon of postprandial somnolence—in colloquial terms, the "food coma." Studies have shown that human beings have a propensity toward sleep in the early afternoon (around 1:00 p.m.) due to natural circadian rhythm cycles. For this reason, many cultures adopted the afternoon nap as a habit rather than a nuisance. In fact, the Prophet ﷺ himself practiced the afternoon nap.[114] Though its specifics remain a bit of a mystery, postprandial somnolence generally occurs because large meals rich in protein and carbohydrates contribute to a longer activation of the parasympathetic system (the "rest and digest" system), contributing to the release of hormones that contribute to sleepiness. When combined with the circadian rhythm, lunchtime naturally leads to a decrease in

---

[113] Mayo Clinic Staff, "Water: How much should you drink every day?" https://www.mayoclinic.org/healthy-lifestyle/nutrition-and-healthy-eating/in-depth/water/art-20044256. Sept. 06, 2017
[114] *Sahih al-Bukhari* #6281

productivity due to the body's natural inclination toward sleep.

If time is available, it is advisable to take a nap as it not only divides the day in half, but it also refreshes the spirit to endure studying for a longer period of time without fearing fatigue. If you struggle and want to use this time productively for your studies (because of your schedule), there are a few strategies you can use to combat this phenomenon. These strategies include, but are not limited to, grabbing a cup of coffee (of a reasonable amount), eating earlier than 1:00 p.m., and eating smaller portions of foods such as whole wheat, beans, fruits, and non-starchy vegetables, while avoiding white bread, white rice, and crackers. Eating smaller meals is in fact part of the sunnah. Miqdam ibn Ma'd رضي الله عنه reported: The Prophet ﷺ said:

> *"The son of Adam cannot fill a vessel worse than his stomach,*
> *as it is enough for him to take a few bites to straighten his*
> *back. If he cannot do it, then let him keep a third for his food,*
> *a third for his drink, and a third for his breath."*[115]

Thus, if we wanted to eat *more* than our fill, it would be advisable to take the Prophetic advice to eat smaller meals, leaving portions for food, drink, and for breathing, helping us to manage portions and prevent complications related to overconsumption.

In summary, when we take care of our bodies by monitoring what we consume, exercising to maintain its upkeep, and maintaining freshness of

---

[115] *Jami' at-Tirmidhi* #2380

mind and spirit through our hobbies, we provide a natural counterbalance to the cloudy, negative atmosphere that accompanies studying.

THE RIGHTS OF THE EYES

One of the most common mistakes students make during exams is not getting enough sleep. Because they have procrastinated during the semester, many students seek to fit an entire semester's course material into one night. Of course, this necessitates spending the entire night studying, and many students rely on energy drinks, coffee, and sugar to get through the night. While relying on coffee and energy drinks may maximize effective time *awake*, they do not necessarily maximize effective time *studying*. Sugary energy drinks grant short boosts of energy but also cause the body to deregulate, increasing its propensity for fatigue afterwards. The detriments of losing sleep compared to the perceived benefit of studying while fatigued are far greater, with negative consequences that hurt us on test day.

Caffeine is a stimulant that does most of its work in the first hour, but continues to work for approximately up to six hours after consumption. The danger associated with consuming too much coffee and/or too many energy drinks lies in the *quantity* of caffeine consumed. Energy drinks contain a large amount of caffeine, but when combined with additives such as *guarana* and other sugars (and coffee, as many people drink these together), the caffeine content increases even more. Consuming large amounts of caffeine can cause serious problems with our heart rhythm, blood flow, and blood pressure, problems that have led to an increasing number of emergency department visits for energy-drink-related issues.[116] Additionally, as caffeine leaves our system, it can cause a "crash" due to waning levels of the hormones dopamine and adrenaline (both hormones which can affect our energy and positive mood that were initially spiked due to caffeine). These "crashes" may occur at inopportune times that may cause less motivation to study.

Another "crash" to be aware of is the "sugar crash." Most pronounced in diabetics, "sugar crashes" may also occur in healthy individuals. As sugar levels spike, the body releases insulin to bring the sugar to a steady state; if the sugar is initially too high, insulin works longer and eventually brings our blood sugar too low, contributing to feelings of weakness and fatigue. With the ever-increasing evidence regarding the dangers of energy drinks and associated crashes that occur after sugar and caffeine binges, it is advisable to instead manage time wisely through the semester and avoid the last-minute all-nighter and the inevitable foods we consume to help us through it. However, it is worth noting that caffeine can be a part of a healthy diet and not contribute to major health problems if drank within moderate amounts.

*So how does getting enough sleep help us
become better students?*

Surprisingly, sleep is the time when we actually consolidate what we learn throughout the day. In other words (and as odd as it sounds), we do much

---

[116] Mattson ME. "Update on Emergency Department Visits Involving Energy Drinks: A Continuing Public Health Concern." 2013 Jan 10. In: The CBHSQ Report. Rockville (MD): Substance Abuse and Mental Health Services Administration (US); 2013-. Available from: https://www.ncbi.nlm.nih.gov/books/NBK384664/

of our learning when we sleep. Thus, sleeping very little during finals week will not help consolidate what we learn; in fact, it will be a detriment to the whole process. I would go as far as to say that even if one didn't finish studying the coursework the night before a test and had the option of studying it and sleeping three hours the night before the exam, versus skipping some of the coursework and sleeping for seven hours, it would be advisable to skip studying and get more sleep.

This may sound unreasonable, but if we sacrifice a portion of the coursework while consolidating the 85 percent that we already studied, we will have a better chance on test day because we will be able to focus on the questions rather than trying to keep our eyes open. If we cover most of the material but do not have enough time to cover the last portion, the majority of what we studied should still enable us to achieve a high score. For example, we would be less prone to making simple mistakes due to lack of concentration and fatigue, such as overlooking the correct choice on a multiple-choice test because we missed a key portion of the question. Additionally, more sleep allows for better time management when we ac-tually take the test because we'll avoid rereading questions multiple times before answering due to lack of focus.

At the same time, we should be wary of oversleeping, as it contributes to increased laziness (from lack of discipline) and delays our study time. It is important to keep a balance, with enough sleep to refresh our mind and body but not too much so as to contribute to grogginess. A person who struggles with their sleep would do to well to improve their overall sleep hygiene. In other words, they should keep the same bedtime and wake time every day (even on the weekends), avoid caffeine close to bed-time, avoid eating dinner too close to bedtime (to avoid silent esophageal reflux contributing to waking at night), commit to regular exercise, and avoid using computer screens or watching television close to bedtime (to prevent the suppression of melatonin, which interferes with our natural circadian rhythm, inhibiting sleep).[117]

The moral of the story is that sleep is enjoyable, but making sure that we get enough sleep to consolidate what we have learned while at the same time avoiding oversleeping is critical in our journey to becoming better students.

THE RIGHTS OF THE PEOPLE AND THE REST OF CREATION

Islam is a religion that is seated in the heart and manifested through ex-ternal actions. As the religion grows stronger in the heart of a believer, their character blossoms and their relationship with the creation becomes even more positive. But perhaps the most neglected people in the life of a student—religious or not—are their family and friends, who they often miss at important family gatherings due to their studies.

---

[117] Melatonin is secreted by the pineal gland in response to darkness and is involved with the regulation of circadian rhythms. Several studies have correlated a link between blue light in large, bright computer screens to suppression of this hormone. For example, Figueiro et al in "The impact of light from computer monitors on melatonin levels in college students" (Neuro Endocrinol Lett. 2011;32(2):158-63.) and Cajochen et al in "Evening exposure to light-emitting diodes (LED)-backlit computer screen affects circadian physiology and cognitive performance." (Journal of Applied Physiology May 2011 110 (5) 1432-1438)

Growing up, I often heard about someone pursuing their higher education who was studying so hard they had no time to attend family gatherings. Because a few hours (for the gathering) seemed very little compared to the entire day, I often marveled at how much these people studied and the amount they needed to learn, and I wondered if I would be in that same situation when my time came. Time passed and I found that although studying for school was difficult and time-consuming, the opportunities to be with family—whether it was with distant relatives or attending weddings and social gatherings—were priceless and something I could not afford to miss, even if I sacrificed a lecture's material in the process.

Your family is your bond. However, if one is truly busy and cannot attend to their entire family, the two people the Muslim student mustn't ever neglect are their parents. After all, Allah combines obedience to Him with honoring the rights of parents.[118] A Muslim student understands the power of their parents' well wishes and supplication. Keeping in constant, positive contact with their parents, asking their parents for help, and most of all, asking their parents to supplicate for them are some of the key strategies successful students employ.

The rights of the parents are many, and they include (but are not limited to) listening to and obeying their good advice as much as possible, serving them and helping them with their needs, calling and keeping in touch with them, speaking to them with kindness and reverence, and holding them in utmost respect. Although difficult, we must strive to

---

[118] Qur'an Chapter 17 ("*The Night Journey*"), verse 23

practice this even if they do not show that level of kindness back. A student may not understand the bond between parent and child, but when the day comes that one becomes a parent, *inshaAllah*, they will understand the love for their child and the parent's well wishes for them to succeed. Take advantage of that love, even if it manifests differently from what we imagine or wish. Your parents are your greatest cheerleaders; let them also help you in your journey.

Lastly, the Muslim student should be keen to fulfill the rights of the people and the rest of creation, being careful not to exert themselves so much in their studies that they neglect these people's rights. Although ritual worship (as mentioned in the aforementioned hadith) and studying are not the same, they are analogous in this discussion of keeping balance in our lives. Being honest with our employers and doing the best job we can, being respectful of our teachers when we are learning, and having good relations with our neighbors are just a few examples of holding up the rights of creation. Seek to strike balance in life by studying but also attending gatherings and spending time with loved ones. These gatherings are a chance for you to mentally relax, refresh, and refocus. They are also a chance to fulfill the rights you owe to the people you love and who love you.

Be mindful, then, of the importance of holding on to your family ties because these ties will lead to an increase in your livelihood (which includes your ability to study and do well in school). As narrated by Anas ibn Malik رضي الله عنه, the Prophet ﷺ said:

"Whoever desires an expansion in his sustenance and age,

should keep good relations with his kith and kin."[119]

To this point, we have spoken at length about the many responsibilities that a Muslim student owes to the creation. However, the most important rights to fulfill are the rights of the Creator, the One who sustains and grants success. Be keen to fulfill the obligations that Allah has ordained, and do not let studying be a barrier in your line of communication with Him.

A balanced life is a successful life. Many students neglect their families and communities during the years they are immersed in school and buried in their books, yet despite cutting themselves off from the world, many times their study lives remain chaotic and stressful. It is time we try a different approach.

This approach starts with the ability to believe that striking a balance between our study life and our daily life is possible, that it is through this balance that we are able to study without imagining it to be the most laborious activity of our lives. It starts when the Muslim student takes a more balanced approach by paying attention to their studies, but not forgetting to sleep, eat well, relax, and spend time with their families. It is precisely these activities outside studying that enable us to recharge our batteries and study more effectively—usually resulting in cutting study time in half—and that enable us to enjoy our time, even while we do something we may not necessarily enjoy.

Work will always be work, and sometimes to achieve what we want

---

[119] *Sahih al-Bukhari* #2067

to do we need to do things we don't enjoy. While we shift our mindset to focus on the benefits of hard work, we can supplement that by balancing work with the other rights that we owe. But as we travel on the path toward seeking a balanced lifestyle by fulfilling the rights of the creation and the Creator, many of us will struggle and wonder how there is enough *time* to do it.

With the Name of Allah the Most Merciful, the Most
Compassionate
By time,
Indeed, mankind is in loss,
Except for those who have believed and done righteous deeds
and advised each other to truth and advised each other to
patience.

QUR'AN CHAPTER 103 ("THE DECLINING DAY"
ALSO KNOWN AS "TIME")

9

Time Management

Time is an incredible creation. It is immutable, continues in a steady stream, and can be cruel or joyful. Time's value is the same in the physical realm yet interpreted differently by the people. For example, a millisecond may be insignificant to us, but it's *everything* to an Olympic sprinter. Some people use time so effectively that we can only marvel at their ability to do so much with so little, while others (perhaps even us) struggle to get the most out of our studying, even when we wholly dedicate ourselves to it.

From birth to childhood, adulthood, old age, and eventually when we pass, we are in a constant river swimming to the Almighty. As we age and people come and go, the one truth to which we all must submit is that Allah is everlasting. He created time, and we are bound by it—though He is not bound by it—and this in itself is an astounding reality.

We live in an era where technology has made previously time-consuming efforts—such as travel—relatively minor inconveniences. Consider that we don't even need to leave the comfort of our own homes to see a relative who lives in a distant land; all it takes is an applicable device and the Internet. Education also has undertaken a dramatic transformation. In my own short lifetime, we have evolved from using green-screen Apple computers, looking up words in hardcover dictionaries, sharpening No. 2 pencils, and using landline phones to using state-of-the-art laptops and tablets, as well as instant search engines that quickly allow us to access extreme amounts of knowledge with minimal effort, plus, we have the ability to store massive amounts of information in drives half the size of our thumbs. Yet even with all of these conveniences and time-saving devices, many of us still struggle with time management. Whether it is in our daily lives at home or at school, the most common complaint is that we "have no time." Let us take a moment to reflect on what the Prophet ﷺ said, as narrated by Abu Hurairah رضي الله عنه regarding time in the end of days:

> *"The Hour will not begin until time passes quickly, so a year will be like a month, and a month will be like a week, and a week will be like a day, and a day will be like an hour, and an hour will be like the burning of a braid of palm leaves."*[120]

---

[120] *Musnad Ahmad* #10560. Some of the scholars interpreted this metaphorically to mean that blessings would be missing from time, hence the time it would take to complete something would be increased.

So how do we put blessing in our time? What strategies should we employ to manage our time more effectively? How can we use the blessing in time and strategies of time management to do better in our studies?

The first step in developing better time-management skills is to remind ourselves of the *importance* of time. Only after examining the importance of our time and how we use it—in other words, building an *appreciation* for time itself—will we be able to manage it effectively. After discussing this, we will then examine some principles of time management with regards to studying and test taking.

When we take time for granted, managing it becomes difficult. Allah has created time so that we can do many things, but the most important is to establish His worship. When we give time for Allah, He will not let us down. Particularly, we must stop treating time simply in terms of minutes and hours we have *lost*; instead, we need treat it in terms of minutes and hours we have effectively *used*.

When we pray or attend a class on Islam, or when our productivity is lessened due to fasting, we have given that time to Allah and hence effectively *used* it; we have not *lost* it. Trust that Allah knows your situation and knows that you could have used that time for anything else. When we take the time to worship Allah and tend to our spiritual states—despite the limited time we have to study—we do that out of love for Allah. How would Allah respond to this type of gesture? Perhaps He would help in ways we never expected, such as an easier time understanding difficult concepts or a feeling of comfort during a difficult test. We may receive this help because we stepped up to the challenge and did not use exams as an excuse for not taking care of the rights of Allah.

How can we reach this lofty level, where we completely trust in Allah's ability to help us with the tangible realities and challenges we face in life? One way is when we are faced with a tough lecture or challenge, instead of stressing or complaining to our colleagues, we should stop our minds from letting loose, think, and ask the question:

What is the best worship at this moment in time?

As mentioned earlier in this book, it is easy to let the mind loose and wander. Left to their whim, our minds will create many alternate realities and situations that will make it easier to procrastinate and immobilize us with irrational fears. For example, our minds might create a process map that starts with a simple question and ends up in a situation that is unlikely and more stress inducing. Our mind might ask, "What if I don't complete the study material?" and then escalate to questions such as, "Will I fail? Will I get a job? How will I ever support a family?"

Instead of letting the mind wander, we must urge our heart to rein in our mind and contemplate the answer to the questions: "What worship can I do at this moment to help? Is there anything in the Qur'an or sunnah that can help me with this specific task?" If the answer is yes, then you have a worship that you can tie to your challenge. If you don't know the worship, then the worship becomes learning about the specific worship that could help you in that challenge.[121] Thus, when we put Allah first, Allah will make the job easier. If we were to rely on our own ability, we

---

[121] Ustadh Hassan Elwan. "The Balance of Ubudiyyah" Filmed Dec. 2010. Vimeo Video, 29:12. Posted (Dec. 2010). https://vimeo.com/17877457

would further procrastinate or fail altogether, thereby limiting our time to study or inducing negative feelings. Once a person realizes how important their time is, they will seek to make the most efficient use of it.

How does one manage their time for a busy schedule in preparation for their exams or for studying in general?

In addition to trying to follow the divinely ordained schedule around the five daily prayers as mentioned in Chapter 4, the following are some principles of time management with regards to studying and test taking:

A BLESSED WARM-UP ROUTINE

When starting to study, I find it beneficial to start with a familiar routine that will not only immediately put blessing in my work, but will also help sharpen my focus on the task at hand. In other words, it's the stretch before exercising and the mental preparation before a championship game. From our tradition, the warm-up routine is to say two phrases: *isti'adha* followed by the *basmalah,* similar to how we start reading the Qur'an.

Isti'adha is the statement of seeking protection in Allah from shaytan, and it has many benefits for the student. A loose English translation is: "I turn to Allah for protection from shaytan the accursed."[122] Shaytan is the enemy that has promised to try to misguide all human beings. To this end, he will try in the most perceived insignificant ways to misguide people to disobey Allah. One potential avenue is distracting us from our

---

[122] Transliteration: *"A'uthoo billahi min ash-shaytan ir-rajeem"*

studies, for example, by causing forgetfulness.[123] From the hadith, we learn that shaytan can also cause people to feel sleepy and to delay doing things (or procrastinating).[124] According to the hadith, remembering Allah, performing ablution, and then performing the prayer undoes the effects of shaytan and allows the believer to wake up with an energetic mood and good heart.[125] Thus, performing *isti'adha* will help the student clear their mind to study by improving memory and energy levels, and by building motivation to complete tasks on time.

The second phrase in the warm-up routine is the *basmalah*. Translated loosely, it is: "With the Name of Allah, the Most Merciful, the Most Compassionate."[126] Saying this phrase sincerely before beginning the act of studying has many benefits. For one, we admit that we actively seek the help of Allah, the best helper. By mentioning Allah first, we glorify and honor Him by asking Him exclusively for His help, that we rely on His might. This helps us to solidify our intentions and sincerity that our studying is for Allah. Secondly, we show that we are helpless and in need of Allah's help to complete this deed. And know that the one who humbles themselves in front of Allah will be raised to even greater heights—heights that they could not even begin to imagine.

A GOOD PLAN

Every test is a game, and to play the game well we need a good plan. Every

---

[123] Qur'an Chapter 18 ("*The Cave*"), verse 63
[124] Sheikh Qadhi, Yasir. "Pt. 3 Tafsir Surat Al Fatiha –Details of the isti'adha (A'udhubillah)." June 2014. Youtube Video, 18:40. June 2014. https://www.youtube.com/watch?v=pwHPPr9nHDY
[125] *Sahih al-Bukhari* #1142
[126] Transliteration: *"Bismillah ir-Rahman ir-Raheem"*

test has "high-yield" and "low-yield" topics. High-yield topics are those most likely to be tested because they cover important subject material and are relevant to the class as a whole, while low-yield topics are details—sometimes important and sometimes not—that are less likely to appear on the test (and if they do, they are typically less weighted). The skill that most students learn to develop with time is to recognize and focus on studying high-yield topics (again, topics more likely to be tested) and to put less emphasis on low-yield topics. This is especially true for finals, when the whole semester's coursework is often summarized on a limited-number-question exam.

To recognize high-yield topics, focus on topics the teacher has focused on in class. If the teacher spent five to ten minutes on a single topic, then there is a high likelihood it is an important topic that will be tested, compared to a topic that was discussed for only a few minutes. Similarly, focus also on topics that cover multiple PowerPoint slides in the lecture or to which more pages are dedicated in the course book. A topic that takes seven slides to explain will more than likely have two to three questions versus a topic that is explained in one or two slides (which *may* carry one question). Once you identify high-yield topics, focus your time on understanding them before getting bogged down in the details. In addition to recognizing high-yield topics, focus also on mastering the basics. Once the basics of a subject have been mastered, it is easy to layer on the details that will eventually lead to expertise in the field. Remember, one cannot learn algebra until they first understand basic math (i.e., addition, subtraction, multiplication, and division).

STUDY IN HOURLY BLOCKS

A common problem for many students is that they set a goal to study for a certain amount of time and instead study for only a fraction of it. A more efficient approach is to divide your total daily study time into a certain number of feasible hours.

As an example, during board exams I typically set aside four to five hours maximum each day with one day dedicated to rest. After determining a feasible amount of study time for the day, I divided the total study time into one-hour blocks. For each hour block, I studied the topic in depth without any distractions. Once that hour elapsed, I took a *mandatory* ten-minute break. This break was for anything I wanted to do: social media, eating, using the restroom, praying, etc. However, after those ten minutes were up, I committed myself to studying for another one-hour block.

I recommend that after three to four of these study blocks (or whatever is feasible), you take a one-hour break. After this break and depending on how much you have studied to that point, decide if you need to study more or if you can take the rest of the day off.

When you standardize your study time and break up your time this way, you can truly appreciate how long one hour is; plus, how much can be done in one hour, free of distractions. This strategy also grants you a sense of achievement; when you truly dedicate yourself to serious study without any distractions for one hour, you will not only get a surprising amount of work done, but you will also have an enjoyable break to look forward to at the end of each block. Studying in blocks enables you to get the maximum amount of work done in the shortest time possible while preventing mental fatigue and encouraging you with thoughts of enjoying the rest of the day off.

MINIMIZE DISTRACTIONS, BUT DON'T BURN OUT

Finding a balance between breaks and studying can be difficult, but it is not impossible. As explained in the last chapter, both taking breaks and continuing your normal routine during study time promote relaxation and help prevent anxiety and stress. As a reminder, I recommend not se-cluding yourself from your family, locking your doors, or abandoning your favorite pastime during exam time in favor of studying for ten hours a day; this will only lead to burnout and stress.

Similarly, you must realize that you cannot study in the presence of your distractions. If you have your lecture and social media open at the same time, then it is not study time—it is break time. Do not be the per-son who complains about studying for ten hours each day when in reality you were distracted for the majority of it. Use your breaks for your pas-times and your study time as your study time. Additionally, if you study in blocks, you will be less distracted and more likely to complete your study faster than anticipated; afterwards you can tend to the activities that previously distracted you.

PRACTICE QUESTIONS

To take studying to the next level, we have to be able to anticipate what the exam will test. A simple way to do this is to perform practice questions, usually found in review books or on past exams (if available, without cheating). The reason practice questions are important is that there can be only four to five realistic ways to ask a question on a specific topic. If you have already studied each different way of asking a question about a certain topic, more than likely you will find the same style of question (or the same exact question) on your test, building further confidence in achieving a better score.

An effective way to study from practice questions is to test yourself as you learn new topics—but do not get bogged down if you are not yet answering them correctly (unless you are specifically testing your knowledge after studying all the material a few days before an exam). Read the question and try to answer it to the best of your ability. If you answer incorrectly, you will remember it better because you'll be disappointed for choosing incorrectly. However, do not go on to the next question until you have read and understood the explanation of the correct answer thoroughly; this approach will help further consolidate the information for recall. Lastly, try to figure out what led you to make your mistake: Was it because you read the question too fast? Did you not learn the topic well enough? Were you tricked by another answer for a previous question? This exercise will help identify weak points in your test-taking ability so that you can fix them and achieve better scores.

REVISION

The most important (but tedious) task is to revise topics you have studied multiple times until you master them. In other words, it takes a significant amount of revision of older material to not only be able to understand newer material but also to retain the information and use less energy re-learning older material by the time midterms and finals are underway. If you have studied a lecture to the point you are sick of the same pictures and are predicting the next word and slide, you know you've reviewed well. Review after every lecture you study. What were the high-yield points? What's the big picture? Do you understand all the topics? Would you be able to teach the topic to the layman? What kind of questions can the teacher ask about this lecture or specific topic? Asking these types of questions as we revise enables us to be prepared for whatever is tested on the exam while at the same time allowing for easier review of the lecture in the future. Practice with revision, for it is only after hours of meticulous practice of the same action that we obtain mastery.

GROUP STUDY

Studying in groups can be beneficial or detrimental. It is beneficial because a person may improve their studying by incorporating the ideas and habits of other successful students in the group. For example, group study is where I learned the importance of practice questions and identifying high-yield topics. However, group study can potentially be detrimental because one can easily be distracted when they are in the company of their friends, veering off topic and wasting precious time socializing rather than studying.

My advice would be to experiment with a few group study sessions. If you feel that you are benefitting from other people's examples or by reinforcing your own knowledge by helping others, then continuing group study may be a positive studying experience. But if you find yourself distracted and falling behind with your studies, then studying by yourself would be more beneficial; socializing with your friends can always be saved for off time. Lastly, at best, group study should be used as a *supplement*, not as the primary method of studying.

BEDTIME ROUTINE

Learning the Prophetic habits for bedtime helps create a symbolic gesture of closing the book for the day and as a preparation for the consolidation of learning that occurs during sleep. This Prophetic routine enables us to practice mindfulness and relax in a positive light at the end of the day. Following this advice, it would be in our best interest to end the day with reciting *Ayat ul Kursi*[127] and the last two verses from *Surah Al-Baqarah*.[128] By reciting the former, Allah will appoint a guard over us who will stay with us and no shaytan will come near us until the morning, preventing any ill effects the latter may have intended for us.[129] Reciting the latter is also a means of seeking Allah's protection from harm.[130]

In addition, virtually all successful people try to go to sleep at a decent time in order to wake up before everyone else so that they can have more time to work harder than everyone else. Even if they do sleep late, seldom are they up wasting their time or doing something that is not meaningful work. Try to make a habit of going to sleep early and waking up for the morning prayer; in other words, live in tune with the divinely ordained schedule (as described in Chapter 4), starting the day with Allah and ending it with Him. There are other *sunan* that can be implemented before

---

[127] Qur'an Chapter 2 ("*The Cow*"), verse 255
[128] Qur'an Chapter 2 ("*The Cow*"), verses 285-286
[129] *Sahih al-Bukhari* #5010
[130] *Sahih al-Bukhari* #5009

sleeping (and upon waking) that are highly recommended for every student to learn, and I encourage you to read into this topic further and implement as many as possible.

When we have finished our preparation for the actual exam, there are a
few more time-management tips to keep in mind during our actual exam
to score with the highest possible result:

START WITH THE NAME OF ALLAH

As we have previously mentioned, starting with Allah first and recognizing
that we put blessing into our work when we invoke His name will enable
us to perform at a higher level with blessing in our time. When we flip
open the booklet to start the test, we should take a few seconds and internalize *Bismillah*, not just "In the Name of Allah" but "*with*" the name of
Allah, internalizing that we need Allah's help to complete any task and
that we enter upon this challenge with Him as our best source of help.

FINISH THE TEST

Students sabotage their exam scores when they fail to finish the entire
exam. For slow test takers, try to pick up the pace by marking hard questions and coming back to them later instead of getting stuck on them. On
a multiple-choice test, a "hard question" is defined as a question that takes

more than one to two minutes to answer. On essay exams, "hard ques-tions" are those for which we cannot immediately start writing and need more time to think about how to formulate the answer. Chances are if we don't know the answer within two to three minutes, we're wasting our time thinking about it more at that moment. We need to move on to the next question and return to the "hard questions" later, because every ques-tion on an exam is usually weighted the same regardless of how hard a specific question may be. If questions on an exam are weighted differently, then we should focus first on questions that have the most weight and return to the lesser-weighted questions at the end. In the worst-case sce-nario, if (as in most multiple-choice exams) we are not penalized for guess-ing (i.e., receiving a -1 instead of 0 for a wrong answer), then even if we run out of time, we should seek to fill the rest of the questions with *any* answer because guessing a correct answer will help more than leaving it blank.

The reason finishing the test is critical is that questions one through five may be the hardest questions on the test, while the last ten are the easiest. Our score can suffer if we don't attempt all the questions because we were stuck in the beginning of the exam. An added benefit to finishing the whole test is that sometimes the answers to prior questions are hidden in later question stems, inadvertently helping us with an answer to an ear-lier, harder question! Thus, maximize your score by finishing the test and answering every question, even if it is just an educated guess.

RECHECK THE TEST BEFORE TURNING IT IN

I can recall many times when I reviewed my test after it was graded and couldn't believe that I answered a question in a certain way; shocked that I picked the wrong answer for an easy question. What I realized after many years of struggling with this problem was that I could have easily avoided these types of mistakes if I had just reviewed my test prior to submitting it. Oftentimes we are so focused on finishing an exam and we move so rapidly that we inadvertently mark the wrong box for a question we knew the answer to. For example, on a multiple-choice test you may have circled the right answer on your test paper but filled in the wrong letter on your actual answer sheet. On essay questions, make sure you answered the actual question and did not veer off topic. These types of mistakes are easily corrected when we take a few minutes just prior to submitting our exam to carefully review it. Sometimes, we may find that we can increase our score simply by being diligent in correcting these types of unintentional errors.

Therefore, instead of trying to be the first to submit your test, take time to recheck that you filled in all the letters correctly, that all the numbers on your answer sheet correspond to the numbers on the question booklet, and that all the answers to essay questions actually answer the question being asked.

END WITH ALHAMDULILLAH

As we started the exam with Allah, it is only natural that we end with Allah. Before we turn in our exam, we need to take a few seconds and internalize *alhamdulillah*—thanking and praising Allah for getting us through this challenge, a challenge we were able to bear. This action closes the chapter on this test and transforms the test-taking experience from a tasking, physical experience to an enriching, spiritual experience. Approaching our exams in such a way enables us to be content with whatever result we receive, not only because we put forth our best effort but also because we trusted Allah in the process.

Time management is a skill that takes years of practice to master, but even the worst procrastinator can create a decent plan and manage their time more effectively. Even if we cannot perfect our time-management skill, if we take one or two steps toward this goal, it will be more useful than being stuck in the same place. The question is, how desperate are we to succeed? Do we have a burning desire to be better? Do we want to succeed as much as we want to use social media or sleep? Are we willing to change our lifestyles to incorporate worship, or do we think we can do it all alone?

By relying on Allah, planning carefully, making multiple revisions, answering numerous practice questions, and minimizing distractions, we can prepare more completely for our exams. Once the exam starts, we need to strive to be mindful of Allah, finish the test, recheck the answers, and be thankful for completing the task. When we make the effort to involve Allah in any of life's challenges, our challenges become easier and our tasks more manageable, even if they seemed insurmountable at the beginning. Truly, time is of the essence. And as we learn to appreciate time, we are able to understand the general message of chapter 103 of the Qur'an ("The Declining Day" also known as "Time"). Specifically, when we use our time effectively, we are able to collaborate on the most important aspects of human life: to believe in Allah, perform good deeds, collaborate on the truth, and cooperate in patience. Know that this is a lifelong journey that will take patience, and every journey starts with a first step.

Narrated 'A'isha رضي الله عنها :

Allah's Messenger () said, "Do good deeds properly, sincerely, and moderately and know that your deeds will not make you enter Paradise, and that the most beloved deed to Allah is the most regular and constant even if it were little."

SAHIH AL-BUKHARI #6464

10

One Step at a Time

Know that every goal—no matter how exceptional—takes continual persistence and dedication to deeds, no matter how insignificant they may seem. A struggling student who seeks to improve their study habits by implementing a multitude of changes at the same time in their life will inevitably fail to make meaningful change—even with the greatest motivation. This is because anything that we try to change in life will be difficult at first. Multiple, sudden, and dramatic changes are even more difficult because we are accustomed to and comfortable doing things in certain ways.

For example, when we are used to staying up all night to cram for exams, it is difficult to change our lifestyle in such a way that we give up our free time that we *used* to enjoy during the semester and replace it with daily studying sessions. When we attempt to study on a daily basis—even with the proper motivation—we will likely sustain it for only a few days because our body and mind will naturally try to avoid this type of situation (due to previous habits). Our mind may create excuses to procrastinate, such as, "We've succeeded before by avoiding daily studying," or, "We're too busy to be dedicating all this time just to studying." Excuses will inevitably make us start fidgeting in our seats, make our eyes wander, and make our minds think about more enjoyable pastimes.

The irony of the difficulty of change is that life is constantly changing. We are constantly forced to change plans when the weather changes unpredictably or because of sudden family emergencies. We are on the path of constant change from innocent children, to naïve youth, to struggling students, to responsible adults, and eventually wise elders. It takes constant, consistent effort to succeed through these changes, which often manifest as challenges in school or while learning new skills. But as we succeed, other challenges will inevitably arise, and we will need to learn new skills. For example, when we finally master algebra, we are thrust into geometry, a wholly different form of mathematics. Furthermore, it takes similar dedication to learn to ride a bike, swim, and play well in sports.

Consider the developmental milestones of the human. A baby is in a state of constant learning from their parents. Even if their stroll isn't perfectly balanced or each word is incorrectly pronounced, babies are encouraged to continue trying by their greatest cheerleaders, their parents, who patiently wait after each fall and each stumble until their child is able to walk, then run, and then become independent. In a short time, this baby becomes a screaming toddler who absorbs the communications around them to eventually become a child, then a teenager, then an independent adult. This evolution does not take a day, but rather weeks, months, and years of daily development and maturity—one step, one habit at a time. Eventually, all healthy babies reach the same milestones through consistent effort and by overcoming mistakes to the backdrop of their parents' warm smiles.

Just as Rome was not built in a day, becoming a better student will take time and practice. In order to be successful in anything, it takes not just hard work but *daily, consistent* hard work. It starts with taking and committing to mastering the baby steps that are the foundations of the pillars of greatness that will rise over time. Consider that Allah Himself revealed the Qur'an to the Prophet ﷺ in stages over twenty-three years, strengthening the heart of the Prophet ﷺ and his companions along the way as it was revealed in the situations and events playing out in front of them. Therefore, do not rush or expect to suddenly become the best student *tomorrow*; start by committing to a vision of becoming a better student, and then commit to the necessary work *today*. If you do this, the result will follow. It is as the famous artist Michelangelo said:

*"I saw the angel in the marble and carved until
I set him free."*

To achieve your dreams, you must envision yourself actually being able to achieve those dreams. Envision becoming a better student and being at the pinnacle of your field. Producing a vision tied to a purpose— "Why do I want to do X?" —will help further increase your motivation to pursue that vision. Similarly, a sound intention will enable you to produce a vision with a sound and blessed purpose. After envisioning your goal, you must plan the *process* toward achieving that goal. Ask questions such as, "What steps do I need to take to start achieving this goal" and "What changes do I need to make in my life right now?" This type of reflective questioning will help give you a clear, effective road map to achieve your goals and curb any anxiety that may creep from the depths of your mind because of potential uncertainties. The final step is to break down each step you have identified through reflection into manageable *habits*, even if they seem insignificant. In other words, after all the envisioning and planning, it is time to commit to your craft through small, manageable habits that will ease the potentially difficult, lengthy journey ahead.

Habits eventually become our lifestyle, but what we often overlook is that good habits need to be manageable before they become agents of significant change. For example, if a person desires to memorize the entire Qur'an, front to back and all 6,236 verses, a possible approach is to start by memorizing just one verse a day. On days where one feels they have the energy to do more, they can memorize more verses. At the same time, one must also remember that they committed to one verse a day, no matter how fatigued or busy they are through the day. Using this method (and also through careful review and other components that go into memorizing the Qur'an, which are beyond the scope of this book), one can potentially memorize the entire Qur'an in seventeen years.

That number of years may seem daunting, but when memorization is divided into a manageable amount (without worrying how much time it will take) and with patience and perseverance, the end result is an exciting proposition. Had a person never dreamed of memorizing the Qur'an, had they lamented at how insignificant the memorization of one line is or felt discouraged by the daunting long-term commitment, they would not be in a position to enjoy the daily connection they would have built with Allah throughout their lengthy journey. Thus, the journey is just as important—if not more important—than the end result.

Small habits develop into massive achievements with discipline and consistency. Continuous slow gains and slow implementation become habits and parts of a daily routine that lead to big changes over a long period of time. While we are studying in school, our daily grind may not be fun, but after a long period of time passes, we can often look back with a more objective lens and extract valuable lessons we learned during that time that helped shape who we are today.

Personally, I learned a lot about myself during the grind of medical school each time I opened my books, walked to class, sat through a lecture, and sacrificed sleep trying to master the content. Even though these individual experiences were not enjoyable at the time, I now cherish those memories because I learned the value of hard work, patience, and dedication to my craft. These were just some of the necessary steps I had to take toward reaching my goal, which left an enduring impact on my life today. Thus, when we actively reflect on our past experiences, we can appreciate not only the first step to the goal, but the many steps that are required afterwards.

This concept of continuous improvement through small steps is prevalent in the literature regarding habit forming. For example, take Stanford psychologist B.J. Fogg's desire to make flossing a daily habit. He started by committing himself to flossing only one tooth after he had brushed daily. If he wanted, he could floss all his teeth, but the point was that he would at minimum floss *one tooth* daily. This may seem insignificant, but as he explains, even if his motivation to floss was low on a given day, the fact that flossing one tooth was so easy and took virtually no effort would protect the habit from dying, even on the busiest days. In other words, if the habit is difficult to begin with and we are experiencing a tough day, we may be at risk of losing our habit because of the difficulty we face in summoning the necessary motivation to maintain it. Because of this type of behavior modification, he ended up flossing one tooth daily, but many times would easily floss all his teeth (especially on days when his motivation was naturally high). When practicing this approach, a person can then slowly increase their commitment. For example, after one month of flossing one tooth daily, one can then commit to flossing two teeth as a new commitment, and so on, until they develop a habit of daily flossing *all* their teeth.

The last step in habit forming is to have a trigger, and the best way to enforce a new habit is to couple it with an existing habit as its trigger (a trigger is an established habit for which you don't need a cue—in other words, something you already do as a force of habit). In the flossing example, Dr. Fogg's trigger was brushing his teeth. Tying the new habit (flossing) with the old habit (brushing) will eliminate the step of thinking about doing the new habit.[131]

This type of behavior has profound implications for the Muslim student seeking to become better in their studies, but these behaviors are also rooted in the Islamic tradition.

---

[131] Dr. Fogg, B.J. "Forget big change, start with a tiny habit: BJ Fogg at TEDx Fremont. Dec. 2012. Youtube Video, 17:23. Dec. 2012. https://www.youtube.com/watch?v=AdKUJxjn-R8

It was narrated by 'A'isha رضي الله عنها that the Prophet ﷺ said:

"Do good deeds properly, sincerely, and moderately and know
that your deeds will not make you enter Paradise, and that the
most beloved deed to Allah is the most regular and constant
even if it were little."[132]

How wonderful is Allah that He loves our constant good deeds even if they feel insignificant in our eyes! Be sure, then, that no good deed is insignificant in the sight of Allah. The Prophet ﷺ tells us the secret to habit forming by telling us to perform good deeds consistently, even if they are very little. As mentioned before, in order to make big changes in life, we must dedicate ourselves to envisioning our goals while dividing them into more manageable habits that will eventually lead to meaningful changes. For example, one could commit to ten extra minutes a day for Allah outside the obligatory duties (such as prayer)—for example reading the Qur'an—and steadily build upon that to dedicating more time to Allah each day whilst never abandoning those precious ten minutes.

If we extrapolate this behavior to studying, then we would realize that becoming a better student will not happen overnight and that there is no secret recipe for overnight success. It takes one small step—one habit—at a time, until we develop the necessary habits toward becoming better students and eventually masters of our craft.

Thus, if studying for five hours a day seems impossible, set a goal for

---

[132] *Sahih al-Bukhari #6464*

one hour and slowly build up. When you feel able to study more, by all means study for a longer period. But on days when your motivation is lacking or other important, unforeseen events occur, do not abandon or do less than the one hour you have committed to studying. This approach to studying will ensure we won't step backwards in working to develop good habits. In other words, if we set a specific, reasonable, minimum amount of study time (that we can do even in the worst possible scenario), we will be able to maintain a healthy habit of studying, making it easier to achieve our goals.

As with Dr. Fogg's flossing example, creating a trigger for your daily habit of studying is also an important step in maintaining your habit. One method of establishing a trigger is to try to study in the same place and at the same time every day. For example, if we train our mind to sit in the same chair, at the same time, on the same desk every day, we will have conditioned our brain to be in "study mode" when we sit in our chair. It will not be afforded time to think about other distractions. It is important to develop a habit to transform your place of study (or certain times for studying) to be used *only* for studying; if you do this, soon the environment and time will become triggers to begin studying.

I have used this strategy in writing this book. Much of my ability to write effectively came in the quiet library near my house. I sat at the same desk and chair, and after a few days, the library itself became a trigger to write. I could not replicate this spirit at home because there were other commitments and distractions that simply were nonexistent in the library. Thus, changing your environment to an environment more conducive to studying is also very helpful in maintaining habits. Personally, it was only when I committed myself to consistency in daily writing that I started to see great progress toward finishing this book.

Another technique to reinforce good habits is to seek good company. Do not underestimate the power of good friendship. Abu Hurairah رضي الله عنه narrates that the Prophet ﷺ is reported to have said:

> *"A man follows the way of his friend; so each one should consider whom he makes his friend."*[133]

Successful people associate with successful people; they eliminate peers that may hinder them on their road to success. We follow our role models and friends—unconsciously and sometimes consciously through peer pressure—so it is of utmost importance to choose good friends. As Muslims, we should seek friends and role models that are better than us and can help lift our spirits rather than drag them down. With regards to studying, it is also important to befriend or at least learn from people who study well. Befriending and learning from good students enables us to learn their habits so that we can implement them; we can then experiment with habits that work for us and others that don't. At the same time, our peers might motivate us through healthy competition in the classroom.

As mentioned earlier, a valuable habit I learned from group study is to predict possible questions when learning the coursework—in other words, the difference between active and passive studying. Passive studying is to simply read and study what has been given to you. Active studying

---

[133] *Sunan Abi Dawud* #4833

forces you to engage the study material by reflecting and predicting ways in which a teacher might ask a certain question after you have studied the topic.

For example, a teacher might ask a medical student about a certain disease in several different ways. They might ask for the explanation of a disease at the cellular level, the presentation of the disease in a patient, its management and treatment, the next step in managing it (if multiple steps are required in the treatment), or its prognosis. Thus, when one has completed their study of a specific disease, they can anticipate potential questions by studying in a way that explores the answers for all these possible questions. The student will seek to understand the disease at the cellular and macro levels, as well as its treatment, and they will anticipate that the teacher may ask about the disease in one of these ways.

Once a student takes care to develop their study habits, they will be on the path of mastering the art of studying and become a better student. Beyond this, though, when they implement habits as recommended in the Islamic tradition, they will have the added achievement of becoming a better Muslim. And becoming a better Muslim may help them lead an honorable life that is in line with Islam and help them enter Paradise by the mercy of Allah, by His will. It is as the famous saying goes:

"Watch your thoughts, they become words;
watch your words, they become actions;
watch your actions, they become habits;
watch your habits, they become character;

watch your character, for it becomes your destiny."

— *Unknown*

Therefore, do not be intimidated by the heights of your goals; instead, strive for excellence. Break your ultimate goal into smaller, easier goals to achieve over fixed periods of time, and then further divide these into small, daily, manageable habits. Eventually, your manageable goals will pave the road to the ultimate goal. Achieving real change in behavior requires the adoption of daily habits, elimination of excuses, and active engagement in combatting procrastination. It will take time, patience, and discipline, but it will be worth it in the end as you taste success at the top of the mountain and reminisce at the joys of your journey and the valuable experiences you had along the way.

"Indeed, Allah orders justice and good conduct and giving to relatives and forbids immorality and bad conduct and oppression. He admonishes you that perhaps you will be reminded."

QUR'AN CHAPTER 16 ("THE BEE"), VERSE 90

11

Strive for Excellence

One of the hallmarks of a self-actualized Muslim is that they put their best effort into anything and everything they do, no matter the situation and regardless of everyone else's effort. This pinnacle of performance is *ihsan*, an Arabic term that comprises a number of qualities. It is to perform actions to the best of one's ability and to perform them honestly, with the highest quality standards, and in an excellent, complete way. It is to be given something and give back ten times more, going above and beyond expectations. It is to be proud of your work or craft and to input maximal effort every time in all situations and as much as possible. *Ihsan* is usually understood in the realm of spiritual worship. For example, Allah affirms the excellent rewards of Paradise for the people who practiced *ihsan* in this world:

"Is the reward for ihsan but ihsan?"[134]

Consider that if we go above and beyond by practicing *ihsan*, what Allah's *ihsan* would look like in comparison. There is no comparison. The reward for our limited ability to practice *ihsan* is multiplied exponentially by Allah, whose *ihsan* knows no bounds. This concept is further explained in worship in the "hadith of Jibreel," narrated by Abu Hurairah رضي الله عنه where the Prophet ﷺ said:

"... The man again asked, 'O Allah's Messenger (ﷺ) What is Ihsan?' The Prophet (ﷺ) said, 'Ihsan is to worship Allah as if you see Him, and although you do not see Him, (take it for granted that) Allah sees you.'"[135]

The scholars have divided *ihsan* into three levels, of which *ihsan* with Allah via the ritual worship is the first (and highest). But there is also the *ihsan* in our relationships with people and our relationships with the rest of creation (and expanding to all things, animate and inanimate). When we extrapolate this concept further, we find that if we were to practice *ihsan* in all things—within and not just exclusive to worship—it would create a harmonious drive toward striving for excellence that would give legendary motivation to complete any task. As mentioned prior, when we intend to worship via our studies and our jobs, *ihsan* would be to study as

---

[134] Qur'an Chapter 55 ("*The Beneficent*"), verse 60
[135] *Sahih al-Bukhari* #50, part of a longer narration

if Allah were watching us study; with that type of audience and motivation, we would naturally be inclined to study better. This is akin to the child studying better when their parents or teachers are watching them, and to Allah is the greatest example.

However, we now live in a time when we are rewarded for taking the short-cut approach—even if it compromises ethical and moral grounds—as the standard toward striving to achieve a goal. The idea of "the ends justify the means" has corroded our moral-ethical framework and has resulted in elevating many people to new heights in their careers, though they remain unhappy despite achieving what they strove for. When contrasted with the people who work for Allah and do their best, even if they do not achieve the same level of temporal success that their peers did, their attitude of gratefulness and joy in knowing they worked to the best of their ability is a means to maintaining happiness. At the same time, there are others who belittle their innate ability—sometimes because of how difficult the goal is—and settle for less; as a result, they work less because they feel they inherently cannot succeed. This mentality also contributes to feelings of unhappiness and a lack of long-term fulfillment, and it is in contrast to the character of a Muslim who should aim to be the best.

In his book *Better*, Dr. Atul Gawande describes the idea of becoming a "positive deviant," which is very similar to our present discussion on *ihsan*. Positive deviants are people in communities who, despite having the same challenges and having access to the same resources as everyone else, are able to implement certain behaviors that enable them to find better solutions to problems than their colleagues.[136] From an Islamic perspective, striving for excellence in the milieu of people who are content with mediocrity is an example of a characteristic of a positive deviant. In other words, we as Muslims must strive to fulfill our roles—as students, family members, businesspeople, or members of the working class—with the utmost sincerity, honesty, and excellence, even if the majority do not.

Many times, we are negatively affected by our peers who do less work and achieve the same results that we do. While on the surface this appears to be intelligent (why would someone work hard when we get compensated the same?), this type of mentality is toxic and causes unhappiness and compromised performance. In reality, our personal growth is greatly enhanced when we commit to work because of its inherent importance, the value of our contributions, and the hope of good results, not just the compensation.

During my training, my mentors were adept at identifying both "lazy" and "hardworking" residents. At the end of three years, most residents graduate and find respectable jobs across the country. However, hidden in the job contract is the fact that the hardworking residents were the ones who received better training. This is because when a hardworking resident took over a patient care team, they worked doubly hard to make up ground and think about other plausible causes for the patient's illness, as well as other potential routes for treatment. Even though it created more work for the resident, they were able to learn better patient care and

---

[136] Definition via Positive Deviance Initiative, https://positivedeviance.org/, 2017

practice more in line with the goals of medicine (i.e., to do no harm). It is also beneficial to note that the patients we cared for knew which doctors gave them their best effort and which were doing a lesser job. Be aware, then, that every teacher, supervisor, and parent is aware of the same behaviors of their students, employees, and children.

Even though hardworking residents worked harder and sacrificed more time, they simultaneously benefited the most because they took advantage of their training the most, gaining valuable clinical experience and, in turn, becoming better physicians. And because their happiness was tied to the *value* of the medical care they gave their patients—in eliciting a patient's smile and bringing about symptomatic improvement—it didn't bother them that they worked an hour longer after their colleagues had already left.

The main reason we must strive for excellence in *all things* is not only because it provides short- and long-term benefits, but it is highly encouraged by Allah, as He says:

> *"Indeed, Allah orders justice and ihsan and giving to*
> *relatives and forbids immorality and bad conduct and*
> *oppression. He admonishes you that perhaps you will be*
> *reminded."*[137]

Allah explains that the bare minimum required from all human beings is to treat everyone and everything with justice; going beyond justice

---

[137] Qur'an Chapter 16 ("*The Bee*"), verse 90

and what is recommended, however, is to treat everyone and everything with *ihsan*.[138] *Ihsan* with people is to go the extra mile, treating those who are kind to us and those who are rude to us with respect, honor, and dignity. For the student, *ihsan* is to give proper time, attention, and respect to their studies; it is to transform their mentality regarding education from "simply getting by" to striving for excellence.

Furthermore, the companion Shaddad ibn Aws رضي الله عنه reported that the Prophet ﷺ said:

> *"Verily Allah has prescribed ihsan in all things. Thus if you*
> *kill, kill well; and if you slaughter, slaughter well. Let each*
> *one of you sharpen his blade and let him spare suffering to the*
> *animal he slaughters."*[139]

In this hadith, the Prophet ﷺ explains that Allah has encouraged the practice of *ihsan* in *everything*, and this may be difficult because *ihsan* requires patience. It requires constant reflection on our actions, contemplating the best way to perform and improve actions with consideration that those actions fall in line with our identity as Muslims. For the student, it is to ask, "What can I do to become better in my studies?" Moreover, *ihsan* does not stop at the peak of the mountain, like when a student becomes valedictorian of their class. It is a lifestyle. It is to imagine new heights (perhaps ones not even considered yet) and to aim even higher, to never

---

[138] Ustadh Khan, Nouman A. "08. An-Nahl (Ayah 89-93) – A Concise Commentary." Oct. 2016. BayinnahTV, 19:13.
[139] *Sahih Muslim* #1955. The translation provided is from *40 Hadith Nawawi* #17.

be satisfied with where we are, always searching for someone who is better and challenging our own selves to be better. *Ihsan* is the recipe used by the great champions in all fields, be it medicine, martial arts, sports, science, leadership, social justice, etc.

Because *ihsan* is prescribed in all things, this includes our relationships with people and certain actions we may not associate with excellence. It can be argued that *ihsan* with people is easy to commit to when dealing with people that are friendly and kind to us; it takes patience and perseverance, however, to practice *ihsan* with people who are rude to us or when we undergo one of life's major tests.

To illustrate the scope of *ihsan*, the Prophet ﷺ explains that it is prescribed even when slaughtering an animal and in times of war. As Muslims, having to carry out brutal actions—like slaughtering an animal or participating in a war—does not preclude us from doing them with *ihsan*. In other words, we must always strive to act with honor and dignity, exerting ourselves to prevent unnecessary torment or pain.

Specifically in war, Muslims are commanded not to mutilate bodies, not to kill women and children, and not to kill via burning.[140] With regard to animal slaughter, Muslims do not treat animals inhumanely by abusing them, starving them, or sharpening blades in front of them; instead, we perform it quickly, humanely, and with the least amount of suffering. Thus, the Prophet ﷺ uses these examples to exemplify that Muslims know that in *every* situation—even in situations in which emotions may take

---

[140] This is in stark contrast to the so-called "Islamic State" and other groups that commit violent acts against innocent people in the name of Islam, whose brutality knows no end, have no concept of honor and dignity in battle, and truly have a distorted view of Islam.

over their heart and potentially cloud judgement—they are reminded to commit to *ihsan*, guiding them to perform every action in a dignified manner.

It is worthwhile then for us to examine this concept and apply it to our lives as students. As we have mentioned, *ihsan* requires that the doer completes an action sincerely, completely and without any shortcuts, honorably, and correctly. Why is this important? Because becoming a better student and achieving better results are in direct correlation to the *quality* of study as opposed to the *quantity* of study.

For example, a student may focus only on "getting by," studying for hours just before the exam only to forget what was learned by the next week without making any meaningful gains. When we compare this to the student who studies carefully and seeks genuine learning, they may make gains in a fairly shorter amount of time while actually retaining what they learned. The same contrast can be seen in a body builder who works out with poor form only a few weeks before a competition versus a body builder who paces themselves, places emphasis on proper form and working out the correct muscle groups, and pays special attention to their diet months before the competition; the second one will always have better gains.

Along these lines, when a Muslim does a subpar job, they should reflect inwardly to unearth reasons for their behavior and seek to rectify their actions. Adopting this habit enables striving for excellence to become the norm, rather than the exception. A person who continually strives against their desires to procrastinate and to be lazy, turning their face instead to the path of becoming better, lives a life of responsibility and upright character.

A person who strives for excellence is not satisfied until their product is of the highest quality. They would not cheat on their exam by copying off another person's test. They would volunteer to be the team leader during group projects rather than try to get credit for the team effort while doing the least amount of work. A student who practices *ihsan* in their studies will not only study to pass exams or obtain a career, but they will study to actually *learn* the material, implement it if possible, understand it, and teach it.

Finally, a worshipper who implements *ihsan* as much as they can will continue to improve their prayer, patience, intention, and relationships with their peers and family. They would try their best to perform extra deeds of worship instead of saying "it's just sunnah." When a person applies *ihsan* to all things, they transform into a truly powerful, formidable force that will leave indelible, positive change wherever they go and upon whomever they meet, toward creating a lasting positive legacy. This is because when a person works excellently for the sake of Allah, the result is that Allah loves them, and that love descends to the people. And we are well aware that people naturally love the practitioners of excellence, which is why we naturally gravitate to people who are masters of their fields, crafts, or sports.

As an intern during residency, I learned many examples of *ihsan* in our work—that going the extra mile and doing things that no one else does improves patient care. If a patient did not bring their medications for review (the quantity of medications is sometimes in the double digits), we didn't report that they "don't know their medications" or regurgitate old medications that are present but have not been updated in the electronic

medical record; rather, we called their pharmacy and reviewed their medications and fill dates (to identify if they had been picked up and were
actually on the medications). I observed colleagues responsibly taking
ownership of their patients by staying late to perform crucial procedures,
not because they needed to sign off on them for proficiency, but to make
sure the patient receives the proper care and also not to burden the next
shift with more work. And I observed attending physicians continue to
read and learn, not just within their field but even outside their scope, to
gain a better understanding of a specialist's recommendations and to teach
us the value of expanding our curiosity and improving our knowledge
base.

Indeed, *ihsan* in medicine extends to how we interact with our staff,
our patients, and their family members. It is to take the time to sit—not
stand—when delivering bad news. It is to shake hands and make eye contact, to use language that is easy to understand (e.g., saying "stomach pain"
rather than "abdominal pain"), to break down difficult concepts into simple terms (e.g., saying "your diabetes has spread to your eyes" rather than
saying "you have diabetic retinopathy"), and to phone a patient's family
member to let them know how their loved one with dementia (who cannot make their needs known or understand how they are feeling) is doing.
These are the physicians that became my role models and the ones that I
strive to emulate, setting a standard for excellence that can be further cul-
tivated.

Further, positive role modeling and shaping a lasting legacy is an important concept in Islam, but one that is sometimes overlooked. After all,
as students we are usually focused on our own legacy rather than the next

generation's. But pondering about the next generation is just as important as our own legacy because the actions and decisions we make now will have a direct impact on the next generation. Consider the example of Prophet Abraham عليه السلام, a remarkable visionary who knew the importance of legacy building. When Allah appointed him as a leader among mankind, he could have mentioned his thanks or for help in committing to this action, however, he immediately asked:

"And of my descendants?"[141]

Prophet Abraham عليه السلام knew the burden of leadership and wanted to make sure that his offspring would be upright and follow his example. Though Allah did not extend this honor to *all* the descendants of Prophet Abraham عليه السلام, He did raise many Prophets among his nation. And it was through the *dua'* of Prophet Abraham عليه السلام that he asked Allah to make the city of Makkah a peaceful, prosperous city, to make him and his son upright Muslims (as they finished building the *ka'bah*), and to extend at least this honor to some of his descendants and to accept their repentance. It is through the persistence and care of a concerned father for his offspring that he then asked:

"Our Lord, and send among them a messenger from
themselves who will recite to them Your verses and teach
them the Book and wisdom and purify them. Indeed, You

---

[141] Qur'an Chapter 2 (*"The Cow"*), part of verse 124

are the Exalted in Might, the Wise.[142]

This *dua'* was answered centuries later in the person of the Prophet Muhammad ﷺ, who recited the words of Allah in the Qur'an, explained it through his actions and deeds (i.e., sunnah), and purified the people with it. Therefore, every Muslim must be very keen to contribute to this blessed legacy, and it is up to all of us to maintain the light of belief and pass it to the later generations.

Thus, it follows that role modeling is one of the best ways to maintain this legacy. Ensuring that good habits pass from generation to generation and that mistakes are learned from and corrected takes careful dedication and thought. Being an excellent role model is also important as a student. It is vital that senior students aid, guide, and tutor underclassmen, not only because they will be their fellow colleagues in the future, but wishing good for fellow Muslims is highly commendable. It is important for the community to stay together and extract the positives each person carries within them to make each individual stand out so that the community stands out as a whole. No one person can bring about change or success to a community on their own; we all need each other and our different skill sets to complete the picture while simultaneously passing the baton to the next generation to continue to elevate the legacy left behind. Reflect on the example you set for your underclassmen; they will be either en-riched or reduced because of it.

One of the best ways to aid underclassmen or your own colleagues is

---

[142] Qur'an Chapter 2 ("*The Cow*"), verse 129

to become a teacher (which may also elevate your own grades). Many students regularly need additional guidance outside the classroom and beyond the textbook, and this is a role we can assume as students when we are doing well in a class. Teaching a topic indicates that one has mastered it, but teaching struggling students will help *preserve* mastery of the subject. I understand taking time to teach someone a topic is difficult (often it means sacrificing time already in short supply), but be sure that it is a wise investment.

By teaching, you will not only come to understand the topic better, but you will also receive additional help from Allah because you have relieved the worry of your fellow Muslim. Treat your mastery as a blessing and seek to thank Allah by relieving the stress of a struggling student—stress brought on by their inability to understand the concepts needed to pass the course—through your ability to teach them. Therefore, do not hide the secrets to success; instead, share them widely. We should not belittle the potential role that Allah has given us in a person's life as their helper; it could be the very means to our own salvation. Abu Hurairah رضي الله عنه narrates that the Prophet ﷺ is reported to have said:

> *"He who alleviates the suffering of a brother out of the*
> *sufferings of the world, Allah would alleviate his suffering*
> *from the sufferings of the Day of Resurrection, and he who*
> *finds relief for one who is hard-pressed, Allah would make*
> *things easy for him in the Hereafter, and he who conceals (the*
> *faults) of a Muslim, Allah would conceal his faults in the*
> *world and in the Hereafter. Allah is at the back of a servant so*

long as the servant is at the back of his brother, and he who treads the path in search of knowledge, Allah would make that path easy, leading to Paradise for him and those persons who assemble in the house among the houses of Allah (mosques) and recite the Book of Allah and they learn and teach the Qur'an (among themselves) there would descend upon them tranquility and mercy would cover them and the angels would surround them and Allah mentions them in the presence of those near Him, and he who is slow-paced in doing good deeds, his (high) lineage does not make him go ahead.[143]

Additionally, assuming an active role in teaching is a means to emulate the blessed example of the Prophet ﷺ, the greatest teacher to mankind. If you doubt your ability to teach, then learn from the habits of the Prophet ﷺ and how he taught. Implementing his teaching method will help you cultivate a mentality of rising to new heights and contributing to a more meaningful sense of brotherhood. The following qualities of a good teacher are extracted from the sunnah and are provided as a reminder for the author and reader[144]:

1.   Desire for your students to learn and sincerely hope that they do well.

2.   Teach with kindness, patience, and forbearance.

---

[143] *Sahih Muslim #2699*
[144] Sheikh Abdul Bary Yahya. "Al-Maghrib Chain of Command." Seminar. Anaheim, CA. June 2009

3. Speak to every student as if they are your best student.

4. Be mindful of how you speak and what advice you give to certain people.[145]

5. Take full advantage of the fact that a student is in a position to learn when they ask a question, and give them more information than they asked for.[146]

6. Repeat information as it helps catch attention and solidify the topic.

7. Teach and remind students of a specific lesson in certain appropriate settings; it helps to associate learning something new with a memory of a certain place.

8. Ask questions to help facilitate active learning.

9. Speak slowly and with clarity.

In short, the point is to help yourself in your pursuit of learning by helping your fellow colleagues via teaching and being available for help.

Alas, when people advance in their studies with excellence and reach new heights in their respected fields (or, for our purposes, become excellent students at the top of their class) a new test arises for which every successful person should be prepared. Anyone with an ounce of success is vulnerable to personality changes that may lead to arrogance, thereby spoiling their success. Therefore, the Muslim student should take great

---

[145] Some people make mistakes out of innocence, others out of arrogance. Some people benefit through listening, others through visual diagrams.

[146] For example, when the Prophet ﷺ was asked if seawater could be used for ritual cleansing, after answering the question, he added that everything from the sea is permissible to eat (*Muwatta Malik* Book 2, Hadith 42).

precautions so that their career will not be the end of their upright moral character. ʿAbdullah ibn Masʿud رضي الله عنه reported that the Prophet ﷺ said:

> *"He who has in his heart the weight of a mustard seed of pride*
> *shall not enter Paradise. A person (amongst his hearers) said:*
> *'Verily a person loves that his dress should be fine, and his*
> *shoes should be fine.' He (the Holy Prophet) remarked: 'Verily,*
> *Allah is Graceful and He loves Grace. Pride is disdaining the*
> *truth (out of self-conceit) and contempt for the people.'"[147]*

If we reflect on the life of the Prophet ﷺ, we will quickly realize that arrogance is in direct opposition with the spirit of Islam. The Prophet's ﷺ journey from the most honored among his people to being mocked and boycotted until he was driven out of his own city, to later becoming the head of state and eventually uniting much of Arabia under a single authority did not change his personality. His personality did not change based on his circumstances or situation. He was not hopeless in times of despair, and he abstained from abusing his power to subjugate the people when he was a leader. Instead, he worked tirelessly with honor, dignity, and *ihsan* to complete his mission. At the same time, he constantly worried about the next generation of his community and made numerous, persistent supplications for their guidance and success, just like his forefather Prophet Abraham عليه السلام before him. The Prophet ﷺ even went so far

---

[147] *Sahih Muslim* #91

as to save one of his most precious gifts from Allah—the immediate, guaranteed answer to a supplication—for *our* sake, as intercession, on the Day of Judgment.[148] Peace and blessings upon the Prophet ﷺ: a pillar of excellence!

In summary, as we advance in our studies and careers—striving for excellence within them—we should be mindful of looking after the next generation and protect our personalities from the poison of arrogance.

Concurrently, we should not be so afraid of arrogance that we hide our credentials so that the people would not benefit from them. There is a fine line between having positive self-image and being arrogant, but both reminding ourselves of the power of Allah and constantly renewing our intentions help us to steer clear of any potential negative consequences. We should take pride in our work and have some element of self-worth with positive self-esteem without going overboard and thinking that a letter on a piece of paper or initials after our names inherently make us better than anyone else.

Therefore, put forth the best effort to be the best in your field, and be wary of creating excuses such as "I'm protecting myself from arrogance by not trying to be the best." This is faulty logic. The Muslim student should seek a path that allows them to push beyond their limits and become the best in their field, while at the same time refrain from being drunk with the power that may result from it. Be the best, but exude humbleness and recognize that success is from Allah. Constantly remind yourself that all power belongs to Him, and after each success remember to say

---

[148] *Sahih Muslim* #199

alhamdulillah to preserve the spirit of success and increase it.

How does ihsan translate into becoming a better student?

Ihsan creates a consistent drive and motivation that enables a student to study with a sense of purpose. As students, it is easy to burn out as we toil through long days in the classroom and long nights studying, but it is harder to burn out when we embolden ourselves to a higher purpose: pleasing Allah. Thus, as we study to seek knowledge, we hope for the praise of Allah rather than the praise of people, which builds sincerity. With *ihsan*, we find ourselves paying attention to the details that others may have glossed over, increasing our understanding of a certain topic and giving us better insight into a subject that we may not have had before. And because we strive for excellence, we do things other people do not, things others would not expect.

For example, the greatest athletes are known for showing up to the gym earlier than all their teammates and leaving after everyone else has left. Why? They are already the best players on their team—and some of the best athletes in the world—but being the best isn't good enough. *Ihsan*, in this respect, is to aim even higher. It is to cling to the *process* of excellence; because to achieve excellence beyond excellence takes hard work, as well as dedication with a commitment to working in the most excellent way. For the student, it is to do the unexpected and apply the spiritual remedies of Islam to their heart to benefit themselves both as students and Muslims. It is to strive to be the best and at the top of the class, with the highest marks and the best written essays because it is praised by

Allah. At the same time, it is to wish for our colleagues to be the best as well.

Thus, the Muslim student is not bothered by the unexpected tutoring session in the middle of a busy finals week, because they know that this is an act of *ihsan* that will not go unrewarded and unnoticed. So what if no one else is studying this early in the semester? So what if no one else places importance on Islam while studying? We are on a mission of betterment; it starts at the beginning of the semester but does not end at our exams. We happily commit to Islam and the *details* that are often overlooked but that many times are the essential keys to success and long-term fulfillment. In other words, we don't have time for mediocrity and don't care if other people think we are strange by adhering to higher standards.

When a person pays attention to the details, they give themselves an edge over people who lack *ihsan* (or lack the dedication to work for it). It is the difference between people who strive for average and those who strive for excellence. The people of *ihsan* transform into positive deviants, initiating beneficial change that not only benefits everyone, but which also leaves a good impression and inspires others to wake their inner spirit to *also* strive for excellence.

Beyond this, it is possible that the seemingly insignificant changes we make in our lives in our effort to strive for excellence were the necessary ingredients and the means by which Allah would have mercy on us and the cause of our entrance into Paradise. Abu Hurairah رضي الله عنه re-ported that the Prophet ﷺ said:

"A prostitute was forgiven by Allah, because, passing by a

panting dog near a well and seeing that the dog was about to
die of thirst, she took off her shoe, and tying it with her head-
cover she drew out some water for it. So, Allah forgave her
because of that. "[149]

Who cares if times are tough or if the job is not ideal? Who cares if the teacher is unfair or the test is going to be difficult? Who cares if Ramadan is occurring at the same time as our exams? These are only small inconveniences in an imperfect world. Embrace these challenges and strive for perfection, the ultimate challenge in an imperfect world.

With this in mind, do yourself a favor and aim to be the best—not just for the sake of being the best, but because whatever you are studying and wherever you work is important. Be the best because Allah loves excellence in work. Strive for excellence with everything and everyone you meet because everyone should know that Muslims answer to a higher code of conduct that demands higher expectations and better results. Work with *ihsan* because when you know you have put forth your best effort, you will never cease to aim for new opportunities and will never regret not trying hard enough. No matter how bad things are or if no one else commits to it, cultivate a culture of excellence in your heart that will manifest in action. Be honest and give your best effort—100 percent—to your education, patients, customers, craft, and family. Not only will people see the difference, but Allah will appreciate the difference. Indeed, life is too short to settle for mediocrity. At the end of the day, even if you were not

---

[149] *Sahih al-Bukhari* #3321

able to achieve the pinnacle, perhaps Allah will reward you as if you did because of your sincere intention (as actions are rewarded by their intentions). As the saying goes:

"Shoot for the moon. Even if you miss,
you'll land among the stars."

— *Norman Vincent Peale*

Lastly, be mindful that the pleasure of Allah is better than anything this world has to offer, and He is the best to trust and to rely on to deliver success.

"If Allah should aid you, no one can overcome you; but if He should forsake you, who is there that can aid you after Him? And upon Allah let the believers rely."

QUR'AN CHAPTER 3 ("THE FAMILY OF IMRAN"), VERSE 160

12

Tie Your Camel

When a student has put so much time, effort, and thought into their studies and preparation for their exams, it is only natural that, after the exam, the thought of the result dominates the mind. On exam day, the majority of students hope that their preparation and what they studied will be enough to help them do well, and everyone hopes to pass in order to advance to the next level. While these are worthy hopes, sometimes things will not happen the way we hope, which may lead to feelings of sorrow or disappointment. In this chapter, we learn one of the most profound characteristics of the believer that will not only grant them contentment with whatever befalls them, but also the ability to visualize the big picture, promoting a life of happiness and patience in the face of life's many tests and trials. Specifically, it is to practice *tawakkul.*

Tawakkul is the act of relying upon Allah. It is to trust in whatever

He has ordained and whatever you are entrusting to Him is undoubtedly in the best hands. It is to put your trust in Allah after investing hard work studying, and it entails realizing the result—pass or fail—is from Him. As we will soon learn, trusting in Allah enables us to relax after stressful exam days and opens the door to contentment, even when the result may not go our way.

Tawakkul is necessary to cope with the natural ebb and flow of life, and no one greater than the Prophets of Allah went through more difficult tests requiring *tawakkul.* When Prophet Abraham عليه السلام was thrown into a pit of fire by his people, he had full *tawakkul* that Allah would protect him, and indeed, the miracle of Allah occurred in the transformation of the fire into a source of comfort rather than burning. When Prophet Joseph عليه السلام was thrown into a well by his own brothers and eventually sold into slavery—living a life separated from his father, Prophet Jacob عليه السلام —it was *tawakkul* that enabled Prophet Joseph عليه السلام to persevere in the face of hardship, and for Prophet Jacob عليه السلام to cope with his loss and practice beautiful patience.

Consider the *tawakkul* practiced by the mother of Prophet Moses عليه السلام. A mother's natural reaction to a potential threat to her child is to hold on and never let go, to keep her child close within her arms and within eyesight. But Allah had another plan. When she was instructed to throw her child into a river in a cradle, it was *tawakkul* that enabled the mother of Prophet Moses عليه السلام to comply—against all motherly logic. In other words, she had taken whatever precautions she could, she followed and obeyed the order, and she was willing to accept the result that Allah had planned. We all know how the rest of the story unfolds and the great heights to which Prophet Moses عليه السلام eventually rose.

Suffice it to say, reader, that if you were to rely upon Allah in all aspects of life—including studying—He would be sufficient for you. Simply stopping there, however, without action, is not enough because *tawakkul* is a deed of the heart, not of the body. The job of the Muslim student then, is to put their share of the work into whatever they are doing through deeds of the body, while at the same time practicing *tawakkul* in their heart by relying upon Allah.

Some people may claim this logic is a contradiction: *If Allah can do anything, why should I have to do anything at all?* Allah has created everything for a reason, and there are certain laws that govern the physical world that require some type of action in order for them to occur. For example, a book will not write itself; it requires an author to intend, write, edit, and publish before it can become a book. It is not enough to sit down and rely upon Allah for the book to complete itself on its own without writing a single word. Of course, Allah is capable of doing anything, but the miracles that break the laws of the physical world are the *exceptions*, not the rule. It takes a pen to write an essay, planting a seed to grow a crop, and effective studying to receive good results. A person who commits to actions sincerely and *then* places the result in the hands of Allah is a person who correctly practices *tawakkul*, enabling them to be content with whatever result is decreed by the All-Knowing and All-Wise.

This balance between deeds of the body and deeds of the heart (specifically *tawakkul* in the present discussion) is illustrated in an event narrated by Anas ibn Malik رضي الله عنه, when he narrates that a man asked:

"O Messenger of Allah, should I tie my camel and trust in Allah, or should I leave her untied and trust in Allah?" The Messenger of Allah ﷺ *said, "Tie her and trust in Allah."*[150]

Some students may ask a similar question: *Should I study and trust in Allah, or should I simply walk into the exam room with full trust in Allah?* Here, the Prophet ﷺ explains that failing to tie the camel—or, in other words, failing to take the necessary actions (e.g., studying)—and simply relying on Allah to take care of our affairs is inconsistent with Islamic guidance. We must work to our best ability then rely and trust in Allah for whatever the result will be.

Sometimes, *tawakkul* is the cause for something good to happen or the missing piece of the puzzle toward getting better grades. We should broaden the spiritual dimension of studying by adding different layers to our study routine that will enable us to pass and do well. This includes a sincere intention, prayer, patience, *dua',* and *tawakkul,* among all the other tools we have already spoken about. Perhaps adding a missing spiritual quality to our life is the sole missing ingredient for success on our exams or any other challenges we face.

If we were to practice *tawakkul,* our worries about our exam results and our future career paths would not cause us to stress. Instead, Allah would provide for us from where we cannot even imagine. 'Umar ibn al-Khattab رضي الله عنه narrated that the Messenger of Allah ﷺ said:

---

[150] *Jami` at-Tirmidhi* #2517

"If you were to rely upon Allah with the required reliance,
then He would provide for you just as a bird is provided for, it
goes out in the morning empty, and returns full."[151]

Note that the birds still need to fly and seek out their provision. The similitude is that if we do the same by going out looking for provision or success and work toward it, Allah is generous and merciful and will grant us what we need. Indeed, Allah is enough to suffice for our needs and our wants within the realm of permissibility.

How does a student cultivate tawakkul in their heart?

The first step to cultivating *tawakkul* is to learn about Allah and His characteristics, for how could one rely on Him without truly knowing Him? It requires thorough, sincere, honest reflection on the fact that Allah is the All-Mighty, the Sustainer, the Merciful, Caretaker, the All-Wise and Just. It is important for us to strengthen our belief in the oneness, uniqueness, and ability of Allah by learning His Names; for example, by reflecting on events in our lives when His mercy pulled us out of a difficult time when there was seemingly no other way out.

Tawakkul requires that we compel our hearts to submit our affairs to Allah and leave it in His care. When we study for our exams after long hours and sacrifice, it is to compel our hearts to trust that whatever Allah taught us and caused us to remember will be enough for the test. When

---

[151] *Jami` at-Tirmidhi* #2344

we complete our exams, we again compel our hearts to be satisfied with whatever comes next. We did our part and trusted our affairs with Allah. Practicing *tawakkul* is to realize that nothing more we could have done would have changed the outcome and that whatever is to happen will happen no matter what precaution we could have taken. We are aware that Allah *knows* what is best for us—even if we don't understand the wisdom at that point in time—and we trust that whatever happens will not be more than we can bear (refer to our previous discussion about the ability to bear burdens and the contentment with however *dua'* is answered).

But what happens if we do fall short? We might make *dua'*, have *tawakkul,* follow all the steps to maximize our scores, make all our prayers on time, and work really hard during finals week, but still come up short. We may even fail.

But why do we fail?

As Batman once reminded us at the cinema, we fall so that we can learn to pick ourselves up again. Similarly, we fail so that we can learn to deal with temporary setbacks and increase our resolve to do better the next time. In other words, it is okay to fail, but it is not okay to give up completely because of a failure. In life, we are presented with many challenges and adversities. It would not make sense for everyone to have an easy life and it would not make sense if we mastered everything we tried right away. So Allah tests us to see how we react. Will we blame Him? Will we object to anything except an A+? Will we lose hope in Allah and become arrogant, relying only on ourselves?

Sometimes, our plan and Allah's plan for us is the same, but sometimes they are different. Sometimes we want to go to the best college, but Allah planned for us to go elsewhere. Sometimes we want to stay in the same city all our lives, but Allah planned that we settle elsewhere. Not everything in life goes according to the perfect plan we have concocted in our minds.

Thus, it requires a change in mindset—specifically, to accept that not all change is bad. Change, or even failure, can sometimes lead to immense success that was previously not discernable.

Consider when the Prophet ﷺ and his followers were turned away at *Hudaybyah* (en route to Makkah to perform pilgrimage) in exchange for ten years of peace; this perceived failure was actually a manifest victory,[152] as the Quraysh later breached the treaty and eventually lost control of Makkah and their influence on Arabia. A contemporary example is to consider that Walt Disney, a pioneer of creative cinema, was fired from the *Kansas City Star* because his editor felt he had a *lack* of creativity (refer to Chapter 7 regarding our discussion about things that may happen to us that we don't like, that are perhaps good for us, while things that we thought were good for us may actually be harmful to us).

What should the Muslim student do
if they fall short despite using Islamic habits for studying?

First, they should endeavor to be mindful that they invested hard

---

[152] Qur'an Chapter 48 ("*The Victory*")

work and a significant amount of time to be in the position they are, that there is blessing in that itself, and that they were guided to do their very best and asked Allah for the very best. They are thankful for these but know that, despite all this, sometimes we fall short.

Reflect, then, that perhaps Allah puts us through hardships, trials, and distress as a means for us to get closer to Him, as an indication that He loves us and wants us to come back to Him. If we were blind to the calls of Allah in times of success, surely the times of hardship will open our eyes and cause us to be desperate for His help. Many times, it is only after we have failed by relying solely on our own innate ability or the advice of others that we are pushed to return to Allah, the ultimate source of success. We become desperate for Allah's help, and in those moments we discover a spiritual clarity that enables us to focus and rely solely on Allah's ability. And even though we put Allah last on our list of options, He mercifully opens new doors for us to Him and to whatever we need in this world. We realize that our hardship is a means to something even better.

Reflect on the life of the Prophet ﷺ, on the pain of being kicked out of his home city by his own people and having to emigrate to a foreign city. Despite this painful experience, the Prophet ﷺ was given the later success of building a new nation with seeds emerging from that foreign city. And it was only after this experience that he then returned to the city he was removed from in a position of power and united much of Arabia. That success required going through a period of hardship. After all, diamonds are perfected after a period of extreme heat and pressure.

Additionally, part of *tawakkul* is that we accept that whatever happens or whatever challenges we face are actually beneficial for us and have

wisdom behind them. We may not understand that wisdom until later—
and sometimes that wisdom is only understood by later generations after
we pass away. In other words, we often do not see the fruit of our labor
right away, but if we build trust, it will help us to appreciate the labor
along the way, and eventually it will bear even more fruit. In the difficult
times that we do fail, the Muslim student should also remind themselves
of the optimistic mindset that Islam teaches. Suhaib رضي الله عنه reported
that Allah's Messenger ﷺ said:

> *"Strange are the ways of a believer for there is good in every*
> *affair of his and this is not the case with anyone else except in*
> *the case of a believer for if he has an occasion to feel delight, he*
> *thanks (God), thus there is a good for him in it, and if he gets*
> *into trouble and shows resignation (and endures it patiently),*
> *there is a good for him in it."*[153]

Based upon this hadith, good can emerge from both positive and negative results. If we do well on an exam, it is a reward for our hard work,
and if we are thankful, our success is magnified. If we came up short, it is
a learning experience and perhaps a training ground to build our patience
for potential challenges in the future. Instead of objecting to Allah's decree
by complaining "Why me?" the Muslim student reflects on their short-
coming and analyzes the steps they need to take to perform better. Perhaps

---

[153] *Sahih Muslim* #2999

they need to add a spiritual tool to their routine, seek advice from successful students, or invest more time in studying. In analyzing their methods, they are able to identify shortcomings from a constructive angle and then move forward, eventually becoming successful, whether in their current field or a different one. The moral of the story is to not dwell on what has already come to pass but to focus on the future and build toward it. Continue to put the best effort forward to get the best results. If the results still aren't there, perhaps there is divine wisdom in that. Know that whatever happens, happens for a reason that is beneficial to us either in this world or the Hereafter.

Building *tawakkul* is a lifelong journey. It requires patience and training the heart to trust that whatever preparation has been done is enough and that the result will be good for us however it turns out. One way to strengthen *tawakkul* is to think well of Allah, because whatever we think of Him is what we will find. This is supported in a narration reported by Abu Hurairah رضي الله عنه who said that the Prophet ﷺ said that Allah said:

> *"I am as My servant thinks I am. I am with him when he makes mention of Me. If he makes mention of Me to himself, I make mention of him to Myself; and if he makes mention of Me in an assembly, I make mention of him in an assembly better than it. And if he draws near to Me an arm's length, I draw near to him a cubit, and if he draws near to Me a cubit, I draw near to him a fathom. And if he comes to Me walking,*

I go to him at speed."[154]

In other words, if something good happens to us, we believe and hope that this is a reward from Allah and we thank Him for that. If we are tested or we undergo some hardship, we do not lose faith, but instead increase our resolve. When we think well of Allah, these hardships and trials become means of purification and ascension to new spiritual heights. When we think of Allah as All-Capable and Forgiving, our shortcomings will not become an excuse for us not to pursue closeness to Him. Indeed, it is because of His mercy that we run toward His forgiveness, and as we mention Him and draw nearer to Him, He mentions us in assemblies better than we can imagine (e.g., with the angels) and is so eager to draw nearer to us. When we develop an optimistic relationship with Allah, we protect ourselves from being disheartened by failures, as these are only minor setbacks on the path to our ultimate goal. Thus, our *tawakkul* in Allah and our determination to succeed are further strengthened, *inshaAllah*.

Climbing to this rank may seem daunting or even impossible. However, not only is it possible, but attempting this journey is at least *necessary*. Building trust in Allah enables us to enjoy tranquility in life because we surrender the burden of stressing about matters over which we have no control to Allah. It enables us to prepare for *any* outcome and react with gratitude or patience, granting us the ability to rise after we have fallen and continue to work toward the destination without dwelling on the past. Finally, *tawakkul* enables us to dream bigger. When we practice it in

---

[154] *40 Hadith Qudsi* #15. See also *Sahih Muslim* #2675.

our studies and witness the results, we are able to apply it to all facets of life and elevate our ambitions beyond our studies, opening the doors to more amazing opportunities.

So remember to tie your camel by studying effectively, and then compel your heart to trust in Allah for whatever comes next. Because when we trust the result to Allah and let go of the stress of the result, we open our hearts to contentment with whatever He decides.

"Those who believe, and whose hearts find satisfaction in the remembrance of Allah: for without doubt in the remembrance of Allah do hearts find satisfaction."

QUR'AN CHAPTER 13 ("THE THUNDER"), VERSE 28

13

Contentment

When the restless heart of a student submits to the will of Allah by placing their trust in His decision, they will receive what suffices them: satisfaction with whatever result follows while bringing their heart to rest. When a person is sufficed in their needs and wants in life, then they will feel content—content in Allah's decision, content in their exam score, and content in their life purpose.

Thus, the complement of *tawakkul* is *rida,* which loosely translates to: "contentment and acceptance of the will of Allah in our daily affairs." When we place our complete trust in Allah—knowing that whatever happens is ultimately the best thing for us—then naturally our heart finds inner peace. This is because we train ourselves to be pleased with what we have and do not preoccupy ourselves with that which we do not have or may never receive.

The problem for most of us is that it is often difficult to be content with our exam scores. For high achievers, not only is it difficult to be content with a score of anything less than an A, but sometimes it even causes a feeling of failure. Truly, it is even more difficult to be content when we fail to pass an exam despite the hard work we put in.

And honestly, life is a challenge. If we let it, life will drag us up extreme peaks and down into dark valleys with every success and failure that we encounter. Tasting true contentment—even in the face of failure—requires a firm belief that true satisfaction and contentment do not come from the material but from the remembrance of Allah.

A Muslim firmly believes that Allah is the Creator, Sustainer, and Caretaker of all things. Naturally, the creator of anything realizes what is beneficial and what is harmful for its creation. For example, an automobile manufacturer knows that changing the engine oil at certain prescribed intervals is crucial to the maintenance of the engine. A layperson may not know the type of oil required or when this interval is, but when they read the manual, they can keep their car in good condition by following its advice on engine care. If they choose to ignore this advice and their engine shuts down one day, it would be foolish for them to curse the manufacturer as they would have no one to blame but themselves.

One of Allah's attributes is that He is *Al-Mani'*, or the "Withholder." Usually we imagine withholding something to be unfair, but sometimes it can be a great blessing to have something withheld from us. For example, parents may, out of love, forbid a teenager under the driving age from driving, because they are aware of the teenager's limitations and the potential for harm should their teenager attempt to drive. Even if the teenager pleads to drive the car, complains of their parents' unfairness, or perceives their parents not to love them, withholding driving from them is not only a tremendous act of love, but an act of safety for the rest of society.

Similarly, perhaps Allah caused you to miss your flight because there may have been unsafe travel conditions. Perhaps He prevented you from attending a party, but afterwards everyone fell ill after eating a specific dish. Perhaps He causes you to fail an exam and repeat a semester, which is a means of opening your eyes to study strategies and behavioral changes that will help you not only to study better but improve other parts of your life, or perhaps the delay caused by repeating a semester enables you to enter a less saturated job market when you graduate, or perhaps that failure allows you to embark on a different career path that you hadn't considered before, but which becomes a natural fit for you later. Allah works in mysterious ways, but if we are displeased with His decision, oftentimes it is because we are too shortsighted to see past the present hardship and fail to realize that the present setback is not the end of the story.

There are countless examples of people who initially fail and then succeed and are more than satisfied with the outcomes. If Michael Jordan had given up when he was not selected to his high school basketball team, we would never have been able to enjoy his career as arguably the best basketball player who ever lived. If Thomas Edison had become discouraged and not continued after multiple failed inventions, he would not have invented the light bulb. If the Muslims lost hope after being defeated in the battle of *Uhud,* then they would never have been able to learn from their mistake in disobeying the order of the Prophet ﷺ and become even stronger in their faith. In fact, sometimes the initial struggle or failure is the *reason* for more disciplined work, improved motivation, and the spark that causes us to rise to new heights of achievement.

> *But how can a person have hope when there appears to be*
> *none?*

Firstly, and as explained earlier, we must learn about Allah and His attributes, but then we must take another step forward and remember Him in different parts of our lives. In fact, one of the simplest ways to achieve nearness to Allah is to remember Him. Sometimes, we are so busy with the demands of a busy life—balancing a rigorous school or work schedule with our social, familial, and personal life—that we may feel that remembering Allah becomes difficult.

One way to remember Allah in this situation is to improve our vocabulary by making a habit of mentioning His name. For example, when a student is thankful for their score, they can remember Allah by glorifying Him with the statement *alhamdulilllah* as a means to thank and praise Him. If a student notices that their classmates are doing well, they can remember that Allah is the *cause* for their classmates' success and say *mashaAllah.*[155] This enables a positive, encouraging atmosphere for our communities rather than a negative one in which the seeds of jealousy are planted, ruining relationships and preventing our communities from moving forward.

---

[155] Arabic expression meaning "Allah has willed" as an expression of joy.

Another example to improve our remembrance of Allah is to be patient when falling short and using the statement, "*Qaddar Allahu wa ma sha'a fa'al.*"[156] Remembering this will help us realize that the story is not over and there may be good in our current situation, which will motivate us to try again. Beyond these examples are countless other statements and supplications the student can add to their vocabulary to increase their remembrance of Allah.

Establishing these habits helps us remember Him throughout the day, enabling us to draw nearer to Him, thereby opening further avenues for blessings in our lives, leading to satisfaction in our hearts.

It is also important that we eliminate profanity from our vocabulary completely. It is unbefitting for a Muslim to use vulgar language, as this was not the practice of the Prophet ﷺ, the epitome of exalted character.[157] For example, when we experience a hardship or an event that upsets us or causes us to be inclined toward using profanity, instead of giving in to using profanity, we should use "*subhanAllah.*"[158]

Secondly, it is important to understand that the people of *tawakkul*

---

[156] Arabic expression meaning "Allah has decreed it and what He willed has happened." *Sahih Muslim* #2664

[157] *Sahih Muslim,* #2321

[158] *Jami` at-Tirmidhi* #2180. The specific incident in this reference is during the Battle of Hunayn in which a recently converted companion requested that the Prophet ﷺ make a type of symbol that could cause them to have blessings, similar to a tree they used to have before Islam that they thought gave them blessings when they hung their weapons on it prior to a battle (they were passing by this very tree). Even though the request amounts to a form of associating partners with Allah, which is the highest sin (as they would rely on the tree rather than Allah), the Prophet ﷺ in his reply used "*subhanAllah*" followed by an explanation of why the request was inappropriate. Note the companion said this out of his lack of knowledge of the ramifications of such a request as he had just recently converted and had not had the opportunity to learn everything about Islamic theology yet, and so did not leave the fold of Islam and was not taken to task on this more than what is indicated in the hadith.

and *rida* also experience pain in life. When we place our trust in a surgeon to perform open-heart surgery, we are thankful for the result of having a healthier heart, even if the pain is difficult to bear and the postoperative recovery period is long. Therefore, a life of *tawakkul* will not automatically transform our lives into a life devoid of pain and challenges; it will, however, help us *cope* with our challenges in a healthy manner on our way to contentment.

Thirdly, it is important to comprehend that our present failure is not the end of the story. The story will continue for many days, weeks, and years later. Even if the failure still stings at the end of our life, it is still not the end of the story. Do we think so little of Allah that if He were to test us with something easy (such as failing a test, in comparison to losing our homes or health) that He would not reward us for our patience? Allah is the Most Generous; perhaps He was bringing you to a higher station in Paradise with the setbacks you faced in school.

Fourthly, to preserve a hopeful heart is to realize that Islam is a religion of optimism. No matter the situation in which we find ourselves, we practice looking for the positive. The glass is half-full, rather than half-empty. This breeds an attitude of gratefulness that will increase blessings in our lives, knowing that more opportunities lay ahead of us, *inshaAllah*.

Consider the incident of Ta'if, one of the worst days of the Prophet's ﷺ life. He went with great hope that perhaps the people of Ta'if might listen to his message when the majority of his own people had already rejected him in Makkah. After he politely invited them to Islam, he was rejected and ousted from Ta'if so severely that he was pelted with stones by the people to the point that his sandals were soaked with blood. In this state of pain and shock, and after making *dua'* to Allah, he was given the option of toppling the mountains onto the people of Ta'if (by the will of Allah via the angel of the mountain). In the heat of the moment and with the power in his hand, the Prophet ﷺ remained imbued with a spirit of optimism and mercy, replying:

> *"No, rather I hope that Allah will bring from their descendants people who will worship Allah alone without associating partners with Him."*[159]

And so the people of Ta'if were spared, and their descendants indeed became people who worshiped Allah alone without associating partners with Him.

By practicing these four pieces of advice—learning about Allah and His attributes, realizing that pain exists as a part of life, remembering that the present life and temporary setbacks are not the end of the story, and practicing mindful optimism—Muslim students enable themselves to use the energy of *tawakkul* in their studies and allow contentment to enter their hearts. It enables them to prevent post-exam depression and heightened stress with the next semester. They prepare for any result—pass or fail—and do not hinge their emotions on the result. They are in pursuit of the pleasure of Allah by practicing spiritual tools in preparation for their exams, and because they have tied their emotions to the pleasure of Allah rather than their exam score, they are able to deal more constructively with

---

[159] *Sahih al-Bukhari* #3231, part of a longer narration

potential failures.

But they do not stop there.

Muslim students dream bigger and have greater aspirations. They make a sincere intention and place their trust in Allah, working diligently toward amazing achievements. In turn, they commit themselves to a life of long-term fulfillment and contentment because of the inner peace that results from a meaningful relationship with Allah. Studying to get good grades, being the best in their fields, achieving a noble career, becoming famous, and having many cars or profitable investments are not true paths of satisfaction because they are not the end goal. There are many people who have everything this world has to offer yet remain depressed, even going so far as to take their own lives because of the emptiness in their hearts. This is because there is a part of the heart that remains empty and can be filled with only one thing to give it true satisfaction—the remembrance of Allah. This is why so many people wish to attain inner peace, but so few find it.[160] Allah states:

> *"Those who believe, and whose hearts find satisfaction in*
> *the remembrance of Allah: for without doubt in the*
> *remembrance of Allah do hearts find satisfaction."*[161]

How can the believer—a believing student—*not* be satisfied when

---

[160] I would like to clarify that it is not a sign of weakness of faith or that Allah does not love us to have depressed feelings, and that seeking expert consultation for feelings of sadness, regret, and hopelessness is not a sign of weakness; rather it is recommended when it significantly affects us. The point I want to highlight is that true contentment comes with the remembrance of Allah, not material possessions.

[161] Qur'an Chapter 13 ("*The Thunder*"), verse 28

they use the tools that Allah loves in trying to study and achieve their dreams? Certainly, Allah will give them satisfaction, and because they are equipped with that satisfaction, temporary failures and roadblocks do not hinder them. They are able to move beyond their failures and challenges—they only motivate them to work harder. It may be that continuing to work toward the goal patiently and without losing hope—while following Allah's commandments—could be the cause for Allah to allow them to eventually break through to their goal. Even if they fail, they have amassed so many good deeds in the process and *inshaAllah* attained good standing with Allah that they would be—paradoxically and ironically—thankful that they never succeeded in the pursuit of their goal in this world, because their failure (and the journey) was the means by which Allah had mercy on them and forgave them, entering them into Paradise. Paradise: the ultimate destination of the true winners, who are aware of the importance of taking account of themselves in the present before Allah takes account of them on the Day of Judgment.

But be careful not to let your mind wander too far in its aspirations. Be mindful of the actual process—what you are doing in the present moment—and each day and each mundane activity that goes along with it.

"With the Name of Allah the Most Merciful, The Compassionate

Alif, Lam, Meem

Do the people think that they will be left to say, 'We believe' and they will not be tried?

But We have certainly tried those before them, and Allah will surely make evident those who are truthful, and He will surely make evident the liars."

QUR'AN CHAPTER 29 ("THE SPIDER"), VERSES 1-3

14

Trust the Process

The entertainment industry has indirectly done a great disservice to students and dreamers. Movies about ordinary characters achieving great feats and overcoming difficult struggles in the span of a couple hours have essentially erased the concept of hard work, of going through the most essential labor that we discuss next: the process. Whether it's Simba turning into an adult within the course of a short song, Bruce Wayne becoming the Batman in a half hour, or Luke Skywalker becoming a Master Jedi in between movies, one theme is common: the process of these incredible transformations is omitted. This is in large part because it would not make for entertaining screen time, and frankly, it is the most time-consuming, laborious, and boring part of the story.

Some of the most important gains anyone will make toward achieving a goal—and this includes students seeking to get better grades and incorporate better study habits—occur via the day-to-day, mundane tasks that are required as prerequisites to the goal. The daily walk to class, the practice questions before an exam, the required reading, and the silent moments alone working toward a goal don't just help prepare a person for the exam, they indirectly train them how to tackle *any* challenge in life.

This is the part of the story everyone hates. It is the most painful, boring part, but it is also a necessary part of the story. This part of the story is omitted when we speak about the greatness of Michael Jordan or Wayne Gretzky—the countless hours of preparation, missed shots, and meticulous preparation that distinguishes between *just* succeeding and becoming the *best*. Our problem (for the most part) is that we want to get to the end goal—being the best student getting the best grades—in a short amount of time with the least amount of work. We want to get through organic chemistry because it's not relevant to medicine, and we want to get studying out of the way so that we can do what we really want (i.e., practice in our field). While there are strategies that can aid a person toward this end, the truth is that hard work is unavoidable. Good work ethic will eventually need to be learned, and what better time than in school when it is relatively easy and habits are being actively shaped?

Consider what George Leonard writes:

> *"Nothing in life is commonplace, nothing in between, the threads are infinite. All paths of mastery eventually merge. In other words, there is a reason for all of this, and mastering*

these first will ultimately get you to where you need to go."[162]

While it is important to begin with the end in mind,[163] I argue it is also at least equally (if not more) important to reflect on the present and our current state. People enjoy thinking about the future, but the most accurate predictors of future events are not just a person's innate potential but their present actions, for if someone were to truly reflect on their present state, they could improve upon it and try to improve the future. As Muslims, we are also encouraged to take account of ourselves and reflect on what we have prepared, as Allah says:

> *"O you who have believed, fear Allah. And let every soul*
> *look to what it has put forth for tomorrow—and fear*
> *Allah. Indeed, Allah is Acquainted with what you do.*"[164]

Thus, we should all reflect on our current condition and what we have prepared: Are my current study habits helping me to achieve my goal, or are there obstacles? Are there certain habits I need to learn, forget, or correct? Because it is not enough to have a vision or a dream, success requires change and sacrifice. It requires trusting the process, trusting that each serious hour of reading and each serious day in class will result in getting better. Once we have embraced that studying is the process—the process to get where we need to go—it ceases to be mundane. It becomes

---

[162] George Leonard. *Mastery: The Keys to success and long-term fulfillment* (Penguin Group, 1992), 150.

[163] Stephen Covey. *The Seven Habits of Highly Effective People*, 102.

[164] Qur'an Chapter 59 ("*The Exile*"), verse 18.

necessary. Once it becomes necessary, we allow ourselves to clear our minds of the negative connotation associated with it, and we allow ourselves to be immersed in the sea of knowledge and its different avenues to success.

Many people of the past have been trailblazers with regards to this concept. Reflect on the example of Salman al-Farisi رضي الله عنه, a companion of the Prophet ﷺ. Salman had a yearning for the truth. He was born in Persia and was trained as a Zoroastrian under his father, but upon passing by and learning in a church, he felt Christianity was better and dedicated himself to it. He practiced Christianity to the best of his ability, so much so that he traveled to many different lands, including Syria and Mosul, to be with the masters of the religion. Each one who passed away referred him to another until Salman reached the last priest, who advised him to travel to a land with lava fields and black rocks with palm trees between them because the time for a prophet was near and he would emerge near there. He took it upon himself to travel, but was sold into slavery shortly after.

Despite this setback, Allah brought him to the foretold city—Madinah—anyway (as he was brought as a slave). Salman didn't need to sacrifice the comfort of his home and endure the rigors of travel, but he was in search of the truth and that requires change and sacrifice. He fell into slavery, but this too was part of the process. Once the Prophet ﷺ arrived in Madinah, Salman's life changed as he embraced Islam and the Prophet ﷺ and his companions brought him out of slavery. Because of Salman's trust in Allah and his yearning for the truth, despite the difficult process along the way, he was granted contentment, thereby becoming successful in this world and the Hereafter.[165]

To further appreciate the art of studying, reflect on the example of Malcolm X. When he learned the value of books, he exhausted himself in the pursuit of knowledge through reading. He famously copied the entire dictionary and dedicated himself so much to reading that he developed astigmatism due to the low light in the prison. But that was the process. That process—daily reading and reflection in the confines of prison— enabled him to become successful in the later parts of his life.

But in the process of becoming a minister in the Nation of Islam and then the process of learning its faults, he was eventually led to Makkah and came to learn the true nature of Islam. He could have been discouraged by his past life of crime and drugs and used it as an excuse not to strive for the truth. However, his time on the streets gave him a unique perspective on the struggle of his people with which other civil rights leaders could not identify, and because of that the inner city entrusted him with an image of leadership as he would never sell them out.[166] Ironically, it was his past experience in the inner city that became an unexpected strength in the future.[167] Malcolm X alternatively could have enjoyed a life of comfort as a successful minister in the Nation and overlooked the inconsistencies in its theology, but he chose to put his life on the line in pursuit of the truth. And even though his life was short as a "true" practicing Muslim, the impact Malcolm X left is indelible to this day—but it

---

[165] The story of Salman is recorded in *Musnad Ahmad* 5/441 in his own words (See: https://islamqa.info/en/88651)

[166] Malcolm X, *The Autobiography of Malcolm X as told to Alex Haley* (1964), 319

[167] This is not to suggest that we should use excuses to make our struggles and sins somehow allowable in the religion; we should always be hopeful and strive toward repentance, no matter how many or how serious our sins are.

all started and continued with the process, a process that started on the streets and continued in jail, in the Nation, and in Makkah, and that ended in truth.

The lesson is to never belittle your past experiences—positive *or* negative.

Sometimes the process is embraced in film. Luke Skywalker did shoot into an impossibly small hole in the Death Star to destroy it, but it was his *practice* of shooting small womp rats on the deserts of Tatooine in his earlier life that gave him confidence before the mission. Likewise, every experience, struggle, success, challenge, change, and class is indirect preparation for our future challenges. A successful person recognizes the lessons learned from past experiences, reflects on their current position, and realizes that the struggles they endured were actually *necessary* for them to become who they are today. Truly history and experience are invaluable teachers.

My personal process was to fail the MCAT and not obtain admission to medical school in the U.S. This is what enabled me to study more seriously and allowed me to succeed during medical school internationally. Because I went to an offshore medical school, the chance of training in prestigious academic training programs became less likely. With my back to the wall and the thought of failing again on my mind, I worked twice as hard to obtain the best possible score on the USMLE.

When Allah gave me the gift of a great score, I expected I would have to cancel interviews because of how many invites I thought I would get due to my scores, but to my horror only a few programs responded. As my previous medical school failures haunted me, I frantically scrambled through lists of hospitals and added my application to lesser-known programs. As I put forth my best effort in every interview I was afforded, I put in an extra concerted effort for the hospitals that were more famous, showing my interest in the program and for the opportunity to practice there.

After many stressful months the time came to rank the programs. As I looked at the handful of programs who had interviewed me, I ranked what I thought were the "best" programs based on fame and name at the top of the list. While part of my heart was hopeful, based on my positive experiences in my interviews, another part was preparing for the possibility of not matching at all and having to wait until the next application cycle a year later.

By the will of Allah, I matched into the second-to-last program I had ranked, a program in which I never even envisioned being a part, a county hospital I added after receiving only a few initial interview invites. It was bittersweet: I was thankful that I had averted utter failure, but I was disappointed because I thought it was a lesser program. With time, however, I realized this was the best thing for me. It required me to show yet again that I deserved to be in training, to push me beyond my limits and take my training seriously, striving to become a better physician. Had I trained elsewhere, I might have become complacent—and the positives did not end there. My workplace matched my personality, my colleagues and mentors became family, and it was an enjoyable place to train, full of pathology and hands-on autonomous direct experience that allowed for well-rounded training. I am forever thankful for this experience to train in a residency program in a hospital that taught me the practicalities of a complicated health system, guiding me through difficult cases while helping the indigent population.

Now as I work full-time, I marvel at Allah's plan. Every step was necessary. Every setback was mandatory. The process *needed* to play itself out in order for me to be where I am today. I thought my ability and score would get me into the best program, but I had forgotten that Allah is the Giver. I arrogantly relied on my ability to grant me success, and Allah humbled me. But even in this mistake, mercy and blessing were in His decision. Allah showed yet again that His plan is the one that *will* occur, despite what I thought was good for me, despite any preparation I had done, and despite any wishes I might have had. What blessing there is in failure, in the process, and the end of a journey!

With sincere reflection, anyone can find similar examples in their life in which a mishap or disappointment transformed into an unexpected positive and the means to something better. The truth, then, is that the process is a required part of life, but for the one who is truthful with the process and truthful with Allah, Allah will never let them down.

Trials will occur in the life of a believer. We cannot expect to simply believe and then not be tested to demonstrate the sincerity of our faith. Will we crumble at the first sign of failure and place the blame on Allah, or will we trust His decree and be patient for the rest of the story to unfold? Throughout history, people have been tried and tested. Fortunately, we have the luxury of knowing how their stories played out (at least in this world), which enables us to build our patience by drawing on their stories for inspiration to deal with trials in our own lives. Not only that, but we are fortunate that our trials and tests are not as severe as they were for the people who came before us, who gave their lives for the truth—true, sincere people who maintained their belief despite persecution and ultimately persevered. Thus, trials and tribulations are not the end of the story; they are often the beginning of a purification process.

In short, the process of studying requires temporarily looking away from the horizon and focusing on our present selves and current situation. Take time to focus on where you are and what you are doing, and that will enable you to recalibrate and start the journey correctly to wherever you want to go. Trusting the process trains us to tackle any challenge for the rest of our lives—to face everything and rise—with a hopeful disposition.

Conclusion

To succeed in life and climb to whatever heights we aspire, we commit to uncomfortable situations, difficult goals, and intimidating visions. Amidst all the uncontrollable forces in the universe, choosing *how* to react and developing strategies to adapt are worthwhile, necessary pursuits.

These strategies include developing good habits that are part of the Islamic legacy, a legacy that spans over a thousand years, producing some of the most successful people history has ever known. This is the legacy we strive for in this book—to be reminded of—at least when it comes to seeking knowledge through studying. In other words, it is a reminder of the positive habits rooted in the Islamic tradition that improve our lives as students as well as our relationship with Allah so that we may benefit in this life and the next. Implementing these positive habits enables us to perform better as students and (indirectly) to live more successful lives as Muslims.

Some people reading this book may find its information basic while others may feel it is advanced. Others may doubt the spiritual realm's merit while others will rush to apply it. An argument may be made that using Islam only for our personal means to achieve better grades is selfish, but as I have noted many times, the true goal and intention is to become nearer to Allah. Further, Allah loves when we turn to Him, even if just in worldly affairs (in this case, to get better grades), and sometimes by doing so we realign ourselves on the straight path, becoming even closer to Him. Therefore, why should we separate religion from studying (the latter of which is a large part of a student's world)? Why should we not take advantage of the spiritual dimension and its benefit to us in this world while actively working for the next? Why should we not reflect on the value Islam brings to our lives? This is the balance we strive to achieve.

Most of the traits mentioned in this book are deeds of the heart and mind—internal changes that lead to external actions, virtues that are the means to purifying the heart. These are the traits we work on to enrich our soul, because unfortunately, the soul is often neglected in our pursuit of worldly goals. There are many other means within our tradition that I failed to mention, but the only way to learn and apply them is to seek further knowledge.

Beware, though, of potential barriers. For example, some people may interfere with your pursuit of Allah by trying to frighten you about becoming "religious" at a young age in the current sociopolitical climate. We have a unique, praiseworthy identity in our connection with Allah as Muslims—a rich history of some of the most successful people who ever lived, the definitive guide to become successful in all facets of life—an identity that is worth preserving. There are too many voices distracting us from reclaiming our identity, who may talk down to us and make us feel ashamed about who we are. Instead, be proud; be sure not to sell this for a cheap price. At the same time, have hope—even if you struggle or fail to implement these tools or think that you are not a "good Muslim." Do as much as you can, for even implementing just one of these tools is better than not trying at all. Let then Allah, in His infinite mercy, be the Judge and keep *trying*, for Allah will notice your effort and reward you for your intention and deeds, by His Will.

Once we realize we should not fear studying or taking exams and instead resolve to face our challenges, embracing the art of studying from an Islamic approach enables us to map the route to our success. When we utilize the power of intention in creating purpose and linking our studying to the pleasure of Allah, good things happen. We realize that our potential is actualized through moving forward from our burdens, and we seek the light at the end of the tunnel, understanding that relief accompanies burden.

During this time of struggle, we seek help through patience and prayer, knowing that these will teach us the discipline necessary for long hours of studying. We open the line of communication with our Lord by speaking to Him more frequently and with proper etiquette, believing His response to be in our best interest. We seek forgiveness for our mistakes and subsequently realize that our ability to study improves. We adopt an attitude of gratefulness, further increasing us in success within studying and other parts of our life. We seek balance in fulfilling the rights upon us—to Allah, our bodies, families, and the rest of creation—so that we do not become exhausted in worship or in the pursuit of knowledge. In so doing, we learn to manage our time by His blessing.

We "tie our camels" by studying seriously and then relying on Allah for the result. By being pleased with whatever happens afterwards, we facilitate a life of contentment, optimism, and happiness. All the while we aim for the stars, knowing that all goals are achieved one step at a time. Finally, we trust the process in seeking our goals, embracing both the good and bad that may accompany it.

Remember that learning is not just a means to achieving better grades or the highest score, and it should never be done in the pursuit of fame. Learn for the sake of learning, not just for grades, a career, or to be the best. Learn to *know* something. Learn to serve, because knowledge is service to yourself, others, and broader humanity. Learn because the people with knowledge are not the same as those without it. Realize that every concept contains multiple layers waiting to be uncovered, with every lesson a new one needing to be learned, every accomplishment a person who is better, and every problem an opportunity for a solution.

But the ultimate goal is Allah. We may implement these habits because they help us temporarily with tangible success in this world, but we need to be mindful that these are the same habits that keep us on a straight path to Allah, a path with endless reward. We should never forget that all success starts and ends with Allah—our work is only secondary. We can be the most intelligent or wealthy people in the world, but it is worth nothing if we do not have Allah. If we do not realize this, Allah may grant all the success in the world, but with the unfortunate end of forgetting Him, and in the process forgetting ourselves. We ask for His protection from that fate.

If we realize, however, that our connection to Allah is important and should be preserved, then perhaps we can reflect deeply on our shortcomings and seek an alternative—an Islamic alternative—to studying. After all, it may be a subtle way for Allah to teach us about our religion and bring us closer to Him. We should also remember that Allah has no need for us, we as His slaves are in need of Him, but it is out of His mercy that He teaches us characteristics that are for our own benefit in this world and the Hereafter. Thus, the Muslim student concerns themselves with bettering themselves on the path of knowledge and their livelihood, enjoying the process of studying and being grateful for the gains they receive.

We may revel in the success of achieving the top score in class, but this is secondary to the ultimate reward—the fruit of our labor that we seek—Paradise, which Allah has prepared for the believers, for you and me, *inshaAllah*. There are many paths to our goals, but the only thing that can save us is the mercy of Allah, and we ask Him for that as we are in desperate need of it.

Go for it then. Tip the scales in your favor by seeking the help of Allah when studying, when at work, and in life in general. By the will of Allah, this investment will be rewarded with a profitable return: success in this world and the Hereafter.

And Allah knows best.

About the Author

D r. Hateem Siddiqui was born and raised in Los Angeles, California. He served as president of the Muslim Students Association during his undergraduate studies at the University of California Riverside and as a medical student at the American University of the Caribbean. He completed his Internal Medicine residency at Maricopa Medical Center, where he received multiple awards. He is currently a board-certified physician practicing in Southern California, where he resides with his wife and family.

Index

'A'isha bint Abi Bakr, 33, 164, 171

'Abdullah ibn Mas'ud, 192

Abraham, 80, 84, 110, 113, 187–88,
192, 200

Abu Darda, 87

Abu Dharr, 102

Abu Hurairah, xi, 60, 63, 75, 89, 148,
173, 178, 189–90, 195, 208–9

Abu Mas'ud al-Ansari, 22

active vs passive studying, 151–57,
173–74

al-Bara' ibn 'Azib, 105–6

al-Bayhaqi, 15–16

al-Ghazali, 116–17

Allah. See relationship with Allah

Allah as al-Mani' (Withholder), 214–
15

al-Nu'man ibn Basheer, 72

Anas ibn Malik, 142–43, 201–2

arrogance, 191, 192, 193, 190–94

ash-Shafi'ee, 100–101

aspirations. See envisioning goals and
success

balance, 124–44
diet, 133–37
family and friends, 131, 140–43
intention, 17–18
procrastination, 125–26
reliance on Allah and, 201–2
sleep, 135, 137–40
work and leisure, 6–7, 131–33
work and worship, 49–52, 126–31,
143–44, 233

basmalah, 151–52, 152

caffeine, 137–38

consistency in effort, 167–72, See also

habit changing; studying as process

contentment (rida), 212–21, See also
hardships; reliance on Allah
(tawakkul)
aspirations and, 220–21
hardships and, 200–201, 204
meaning of, 213–16
tools to develop, 216–20

decision making
intention and, 16–17
istikhara prayer, 90–91

depression, 219

despair of Allah's mercy, 94, 102–3,
104

dhikr (remembrance of Allah). See
remembrance of Allah (dhikr)

diet, 133–37

Disney, Walt, 205

dua' (supplication), 68–92, See also
prayer
acceptance of, 69, 73–74, 83–86,
119–23, 193, 204
best times for, 74–76
etiquette of, 77–83
in desperate times, 70–71
in good times and bad, 89–90
istikhara (prayer for making
decision), 90–91
language of, 75, 88–89, 216–17
of Abraham, 187–88
remembering Allah, 106, 216–17,
217
seeking forgiveness, 102–3
significance of, 72–74
sincerity in, 91–92
studying and, 86–88

Dyer, Wayne, 15
Edison, Thomas, 215
envisioning goals and success, 39–40,
    46, 171, 175, 200–201, 209–10
exam and test techniques, 159–62
exam techniques, 159–62
exams and tests. *See also* exam and test
    techniques; failure; fear
  as stepping stones, 20–21
  contentment, 214
  fear of, 2–3, 97–98
  gratefulness and, 161–62
excellence *(ihsan)*, 176–97
  arrogance, 190–94
  in all things, 181–85, 183
  in studies, 194–97
  meaning of *ihsan*, 177–80
  positive role modeling, 185–91
  value of hard work, 180–81, 185–86
exercise, 131–33
experiences in life, 226–30, *See also*
    failure; studying as process
  learning from, 28, 169, 205–10
  not accidental, 119–22
  perceptions of, 2
  transformed into good deeds, 21–23
failure. *See also* experiences in life
  as blessing, 119–23, 213–16, 221,
    230
  as learning experience, 205–10
  fear of, 2–3, 5, 69, 150
  reasons for, 204–5
fajr (dawn prayer), 55–56, *See also*
    prayer
family, 75–76, 108, 131, 140–43, *See*
    also relationships with people
fasting, 30–33, 50, 76, 106, 149
fear
  of effort, 125–26
  of exams and tests. *See* exams and
    tests, fear of

of failure. *See* failure, fear of
of public speaking, 69–70, 88–89
Fogg, B.J., 169–70
forgiveness, asking for, 94–108
  despair of Allah's mercy, 94, 102–3,
    104
  eliminating sinful practices, 100–
    102, 227
  memorization vs understanding, 95–
    98, 107–8
  memorizing Qur'an, 97, 98–100,
    107–8, 168–69
  ways to seek forgiveness, 105–8
Friday prayer, 51–52, 62, *See also*
    prayer
friends, 140–43, 173, *See also*
    relationships with people
Gawande, Atul, 179–80
goal setting, 39–40, 167–68, 172,
    175, 209–10
gratefulness, 110–23
  after tests, 161–62
  disappointments and, 119–23, 207
  hardships and, 42, 221
  in *dua'* supplication, 78–79
  increase and, 112–13
  levels of, 116–19
  postive mindset, 113–15
  sincerity in, 111–12
  success and, 193
group study, 157–58, 173–74
habit changing, 164–75, *See* also
    habits; routines
  consistency in effort, 167–72
  difficulties in changing, 165–67
  Islamic tradition on, 170
  replacing bad with good, 101–2,
    103–4
habits. *See also* habit changing;
    routines
  bedtime routine, 158–59

in Ramadan, 31–32, 50
prayer and, 55–56
Qur'an memorization and, 98–100,
107–8, 168–69
hadith of intention, 14–16
hadith of Jibreel, 178
hardships, 26–36, *See also* hardships
and relief
as stepping stones, 45–46, 119–23,
206
elevation of potential, 33–35, 108
learning from, 28
positive mindset and, 29–33, 35–36,
39–40, 42, 65, 207
purification and, 208–9, 221, 230–
31
hardships and relief, 38–46, *See also*
contentment *(rida)*; hardships
prayer as relief, 52–54
promise of ease, 42, 44, 42–45, 162–
63
Prophet's example in, 41–42, 41, 52–
54, 205, 206
relieving others, 189
hope. *See* hardships and relief
ihsan. See excellence *(ihsan)*
ikhlas (sincerity). *See* sincerity *(ikhlas)*
intention, 14–24
actions rewarded by, 16–18, 24, 197
balance in life and, 17–18, 232–33
hadith of intention, 14–16
making and renewing, 19–21, 20
sincerity of action and, 16, 21–24,
232–33, 220
Islamic concepts and studying, 7–12,
232–36, *See also* balance;
contentment; *dua'* (supplication);
excellence *(ihsan)*; forgiveness,
asking for; gratefulness; habit
changing; hardships; hardships and
relief; intention; patience; prayer;

reliance on Allah *(tawakkul)*; time
management
isti'adha, 151–52, 151
istikhara (prayer for making decision),
90–91
Jordan, Michael, 215
Joseph, 200
Khalid ibn al-Waleed, 23–24
language
of *dua'* (supplication), 75, 216–17,
217
profanity, 217
legacy building, 186–88
Leonard, George, 224–25
life experiences. *See* experiences in life
lifestyle
excellence (ihsan) as, 182–83
habits and, 168
memorization, 97, 98–100, 107–8,
168–69
memorization vs understanding, 95–
98, 107–8
Michelangelo, 167
Miqdam ibn Ma'd, 136
morning hours, 31–32, 55–56
Moses, 88–89, 200–201
motivation. *See also* excellence *(ihsan)*;
habit changing; hardships;
hardships and relief
diet and exercise, 132–33, 137–38
failure and, 215–17, 221
fear and, 97–98, 125–26
friends and, 173
intention and, 18–21
positive mindset and, 35–36, 114–15
prayer and, 55–58, 63–64
warm-up routine and, 151–52
Muhammad, example of
as teacher, 190–91, 191
in daily routine, 135, 136
in hardship, 41–42, 41, 52–54, 205,

206
  in language, 217
  in worship, 52–53, 122
Muhammad, relationship with, 78–
  79, 117
nature of time, 147–48
night hours, 59–61, 76
pastimes and hobbies, 3, 6–7, 10,
  131–33
patience, 50–51, 64–66, 100, 182, *See*
  also prayer
Pharaoh, 71
positive deviants, 179–80, 195
positive mindset
  confidence and, 39–40
  gratefulness and, 113–15
  in hardships, 29–33, 35–36, 39–40,
    42–45, 65, 207–8
  reason for studying and, 8–9
positive role modeling, 185–91
prayer, 48–64, *See also* dua'
  (supplication); patience
  as comfort, 52–54
  basics of, 97
  daily schedule of, 55–58, 63–64,
    149–51
  dedication to, 49–52
  fajr (dawn) prayer, 55–56
  Friday prayer, 51–52, 62
  in congregation, 56–57
  tahajjud (late night) prayer, 59–60
  voluntary prayers, 62–63
  work schedule and, 58–62, 61
procrastination, 2–6, 125–26, 150–51,
  166
profanity, 217
public speaking, fear of, 69–70
purity *(wudu')*, 106, 152
Qur'an memorization, 97, 98–100,
  107–8, 168–69
Ramadan, ix, 27, 30–33, 50, 88, 106,

196
reasons for studying
  as worship, 19–21
  for sake of learning, 235
  positive mindset and, 8–9
  to strengthen faith, 11–12
  worldly reasons, 2, 3–4, 220
reflection. *See* self-reflection
relationship with Allah, 43–45, 203–4,
  See also dua' (supplication);
  hardships; hardships and relief;
  prayer
  barriers to, 233–34
  contentment and, 212–21
  dua' (supplication) and, 73–74
  hardship and, 200–201
  patience and, 65–66, 66
  priorities in, 99
  remembering Allah, 106, 216–17,
    216, 217
  self-reflection and, 108, 167–68,
    182, 225–26
relationships with people, 108, 131,
  140–43, 173, 183–84
reliance on Allah *(tawakkul)*. *See also*
  contentment *(rida)*
  balance and, 198–210
  cultivating *tawakkul*, 203–4
  failure and, 205–10
  meaning of *tawakkul*, 199–203
  reasons for failure, 204–5
remembrance of Allah *(dhikr)*, 106,
  216–17, 217, *See also dua'*
  (supplication); relationship with
  Allah
rida. *See* contentment *(rida)*
role modeling, 185–91
routines, 131–33, 151–52, 158–59,
  See also habit changing; habits;
  prayer
Sakhr al-Ghamidi, 31

Salman al-Farisi, 226–27

self-reflection, 108, 182, 207–8, 225–26, *See also* intention

Shaddad ibn Aws, 182

shaytan (Satan), protection from, 151–52, 151

sincerity *(ikhlas)*
  in gratefulness, 111–12
  of actions and intention, 16, 21–24, 167–68, 184–85, 194, 201, 220
  of *dua'* (supplication), 70, 91–92
  of faith, 230–31

sins
  effects on memory, 100–101
  expiation of, 33, 101, 106
  making excuses for, 227

sleep
  amount of, 135, 137–40, 140
  bedtime routine, 158–59
  naps, 135–36
  prayers and, 55–56

stress. *See* worry and stress

study techniques, 151–57, 173–74, *See also* habit changing

studying as process, 222–31, *See also* experiences in life; hardships
  difficulties and purification, 226–31
  mundaneness of studying, 223–26

success. *See also* envisioning goals and success; prayer; studying as process
  after failure, 205–8, 215–16
  from Allah, 23–24, 112–13, 193, 200
  keys to, 114
  meaning of, 179

Suhaib, 207

tahajjud (late night) prayer, 59–60, 76

tawakkul. See reliance on Allah *(tawakkul)*

teachers, "unfair,", 29–30

teaching, 188–91, 191

techniques for exams, 159–62

techniques for studying, 151–57, 173–74, *See also* habit changing tests. *See* exams and tests

tie your camel. *See* reliance on Allah *(tawakkul)*

time management, 146–63
  exam techniques, 159–62
  nature of time, 147–48, 148
  sleep and, 135–40, 140, 158–59
  study techniques, 152–58, 173–74
  study warm-up routine, 151–52
  worship and work schedule, 58–62, 61
  worship's daily schedule, 55–58, 63–64, 63–64, 149–51

trials and tribulations. *See* hardships

triggers of habits, 170, 172–73

Umar ibn al-Khattab, 14, 23, 83, 104, 202–3

work, value of, 180–81, 185–86, *See also* excellence *(ihsan)*

worry and stress, 43, 52–54, 202–3, 209–10, *See also* hardships; hardships and relief

worship. *See also dua'* (supplication); intention; prayer
  actions as, 19–23, 118–19, 196
  daily prayer schedule, 55–58, 63–64, 149–51
  dua' (supplication) as, 72
  ihsan (excellence) in, 185
  proactivity in, 20–21, 54
  time management and, 58–62, 61
  work and, 49–52, 126–31, 143–44, 233

wudu' (ablution), 106, 152

X, Malcolm, 227–28

For more information, questions, or for speaking inquiries
related to this book please contact:

FACEBOOK: www.facebook.com/anislamicapproach

EMAIL: anislamicapproach@gmail.com

53986930R00141

Made in the USA
Columbia, SC
23 March 2019